GULF'S

FIELDGUIDE

SERIES

A FIELD GUIDE TO
SNAKES
OF CALIFORNIA

PHILIP R. BROWN

Gulf Publishing Company
Houston, Texas

To Barbara

A Field Guide to Snakes of California

Gulf Publishing Company
Book Division
P.O. Box 2608 ☐ Houston, Texas 77252-2608

10   9   8   7   6   5   4   3   2   1

Library of Congress Cataloging-in-Publication Data

Brown, Philip R.
    A field guide to snakes of California / Philip R. Brown.
        p.   cm. – (Gulf's field guide series)
    Includes bibliographical references and index.
    ISBN 0-87719-308-8
    1. Snakes–California–Identification.   I. Title.   II. Series.
    QL666.06B8688   1997
    597.96′09794–dc21   97-13776
                                                              CIP

Contents

Acknowledgments

Anyone who sits down to write a book like this soon finds that it is not a one-person project. Throughout the course of this undertaking, I have had the great advantage of having received much professional help. Among those who in some way or other helped me acquire information are Sean Barry, Robert L. Bezy, Paul Collins, Rob Drews, Robert Fisher, L. Lee Grismer, Robert W. Hansen, Dan Holland, Bryan Jennings, Mark Jennings, Colin McCarthy, Sean McKeown, Robert C. Stebbins, Barbara Stein, Glenn R. Stewart, Samuel S. Sweet, Jens Vindum, and Humberto Wong. Sally Shelton, director of collections, care, and research at the San Diego Museum of Natural History, allowed me to examine Lawrence M. Klauber's collection (akin to entering a shrine for me).

I wish to thank the following people and organizations for providing me with quality photographs, allowing me to depict all 38 species of snakes pictorially: John M. Brode of the California Department of Fish and Game; Robert L. Bezy of the Natural History Museum of Los Angeles County; Joseph and Suzanne Collins; Paul Collins; W. Jake Houck; Sean McKeown; Paul O'Connor; Ian Recchio; Chris Scott of Ecologic Enterprises, Inc.; Dennis Sheridan; and The Wildlife Conservation Society (Bronx Zoo).

Several people reviewed a draft of this text and offered many helpful suggestions. I wish to thank Sean McKeown, Robert C. Stebbins, and Samuel S. Sweet for their generous time and information. Thanks are also due to Kristine Dunn, my editor at Gulf Publishing Company, who graciously put up with my erratic schedule and made this book possible.

I thank my friends and colleagues at the Santa Barbara Museum of Natural History, who knew about this project and encouraged me to follow through with it and offered support along the way: Paul Collins, Mary Gosselin, Renée McLean, and Kay Woolsey.

Finally, special recognition goes to Barbara, my wife, who did everything: Encouraged and cajoled, proofread, edited, offered suggestions and support throughout, and who really made me believe that I could do it. This book is dedicated to Barbara.

Preface

*"In this day of liberal thought and broad reasoning, any
person whose knowledge of the world of reptiles is limited to
the false notion that all these creatures are either 'slimy' or
dangerous is to be pitied."*

—William T. Hornaday, 1904

Interest in snakes and other reptiles has grown immeasurably in the past couple of decades. Zoo and museum exhibits, television documentaries, educational programs, and increased contact with the animals themselves have brought about a wider acceptance and understanding of these fascinating creatures and their roles in the natural world. This has generated a greater interest in identifying those that can be found in natural areas near our own neighborhoods and recreation areas. That is the purpose of this book. As the title implies, it is a guide to the identification of snakes in the field—an aide to looking for the characteristics of a snake in the wild that tell you what it is.

California has a rich and varied topography and climate. Both the highest and lowest points of land in the contiguous United States are located here—Mount Whitney, at 14,494 feet above sea level, to Badwater in Death Valley, 282 feet *below* sea level! From a 1,000-mile coastline to forest-cloaked mountains, from a great Central Valley to deserts dotted with palm oases, California provides habitats for an astounding array of plant and animal life. Among these are 38 species of snakes—more than one-fourth of the total number of snakes in the country—some endemic (found nowhere else in the world) and others representatives of more widespread species. There are desert burrowers, sidewinders, constrictors, two members of the boa family, and an ocean-dwelling serpent that occasionally visits our southern shores.

Many of these snakes are common, but many are rapidly being extirpated by California's burgeoning human population. Some snake species are endangered. All are fascinating and deserving of respect and preservation. It is hoped that by using this book you will be able to identify those snakes you may come across on your journeys through the state, learn a little about how they live, and develop an admiration and understanding of them (even if you never learn to like them).

This is a field guide—take it into the field with you. Write in it, mark pages with your own notes and observations, dates you saw a particular species, and so on. Let it become an old, comfortable, dog-eared companion. A book like this is meant to be used.

Happy snake watching!

Introduction

As mentioned in the Preface, this book is a guide to the identification of the snakes found in California. In addition to identification, this book presents information on the habitat preferences, size, feeding habits, reproduction, and behavior of each species. Status is included where a species or subspecies is protected by state or federal laws or is otherwise of concern. Care in captivity and herpetoculture (breeding and rearing captive reptiles and amphibians) are outside the scope of this book; for these subjects, the reader is referred to Rossi and Rossi's *Snakes of the United States and Canada: Keeping Them Healthy in Captivity, Vol. 2 (Western Area)*, and to the various reptile and herpetocultural periodicals available such as *The Vivarium, Reptiles,* and *Reptile and Amphibian*.

California's
Natural Features

OREGON

Klamath Mountains

Mt. Shasta

Cascade Range

Modoc Plateau

Pit R.

Eel R.

NORTH COAST RANGES

SACRAMENTO VALLEY

Feather R.

Sacramento R.

Russian R.

CENTRAL

Yuba R.

American R.

Lake Tahoe

Cosumnes R.

NEVADA

Mokelumne R.

Stanislaus R.

San Francisco Bay

Tuolumne R.

Mono Lake

SIERRA NEVADA

Merced R.

Great Basin Desert

Monterey Bay

San Joaquin R.

VALLEY

Owens R.

BASIN RANGES

Kings R.

Kaweah R.

x Mt. Whitney

SOUTH COAST RANGES

PACIFIC OCEAN

SAN JOAQUIN VALLEY

Tule R.

Kern R.

Death Valley

Tehachapi Mountains

Pt. Arguello
Pt. Conception

Transverse Ranges

MOJAVE DESERT

Channel Islands

Peninsular Ranges

Salton Sea

Colorado River

Colorado Desert

ARIZONA

BAJA CALIFORNIA

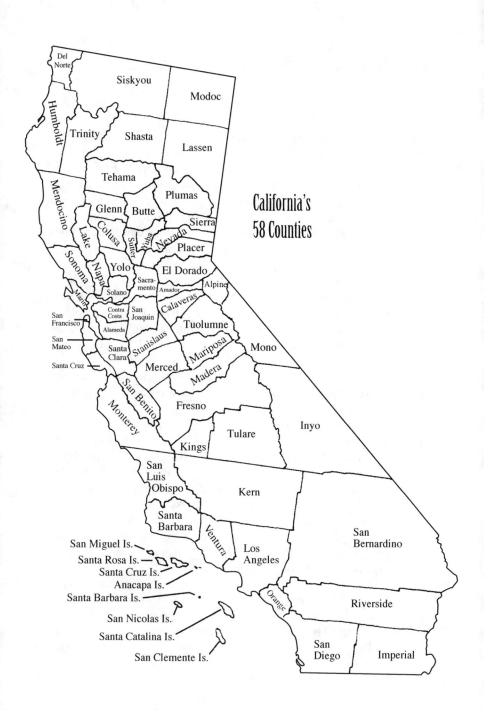

Del Norte

Siskyou

Modoc

Humboldt

Trinity

Shasta

Lassen

California's
58 Counties

Mendocino

Tehama

Plumas

Glenn

Butte

Sierra

Lake

Colusa

Sutter

Yuba

Nevada

Placer

Sonoma

Napa

Yolo

El Dorado

Marin

Solano

Sacramento

Amador

Alpine

San Francisco

Contra Costa

San Joaquin

Calaveras

San Mateo

Alameda

Tuolumne

Santa Cruz

Santa Clara

Stanislaus

Mariposa

Mono

Merced

Madera

San Benito

Fresno

Monterey

Tulare

Inyo

Kings

San Luis Obispo

Kern

Santa Barbara

San Miguel Is.

Santa Rosa Is.

Santa Cruz Is.

Anacapa Is.

Santa Barbara Is.

Ventura

Los Angeles

San Bernardino

San Nicolas Is.

Orange

Riverside

Santa Catalina Is.

San Clemente Is.

San Diego

Imperial

3

Illustrations

Each Species Account contains an "At A Glance" table which includes illustrations of the head from two or three views and other pertinent characters of identification, measurements that refer to the total length of the snake—from nose tip to tail tip, as well as a brief description of the snake. Turn to these pages to confirm identification you have initially made through keying out a specimen. These are not scientific illustrations but merely drawings designed to highlight some of the diagnostics of pattern or scalation that may aid in identification. Color and patterns described are typical of those found in California specimens; wide-ranging species may look different in other states. In addition, the color section contains photographs of all of the state's species, and often an initial identification can be made from these. Like other animals, snakes are variable in color and pattern even within a species, and some that frequently have more variation than others are illustrated by more than one photograph. The numbers on the photographs refer to the numbers assigned to the species in the text. These numbers also appear in the keys and in the index.

A note on the terms "venomous," "mildly venomous," and "nonvenomous" that appear at the top of each "At A Glance" table: The terms are used herein to reflect the relative danger to humans. There are many small snakes that purportedly have some venomous qualities to their saliva (snake venoms are all basically modified saliva) designed to help immobilize prey. These snakes, referred to as "mildly venomous," include ringneck snakes, black-headed snakes, the night snake, and the lyre snake. Although some authorities suspect that even garter snakes may have some venomous qualities, I list them as nonvenomous. In all of these cases, with the possible exception of the lyre snake, (see page 151), the venom is harmless to humans and, in many cases, the snakes are too small to effectively bite a person. In California only the rattlesnakes pose serious danger to human beings. The yellowbelly sea snake is also potentially deadly, but it seldom attempts to bite, and its appearance in California waters is so rare that it barely merits mention.

Range Maps

Range maps are provided for each species, with subspecies distributions delineated on separate maps. Obviously these maps are small and general, and it is important to remember that they only point out general areas in the state where the snake has been found. Within a range there may be only certain habitats in which a particular species is found—rocky outcrops, stream canyons, etc. Many snakes have spotty or disjunct distribution, even within a relatively wide range. The maps are useful in identification, especially in some of the harder-to-determine species. If a species does not occur within the range in which you found an unidentified snake, chances are you can eliminate that species as a possibility. It could, however, mean that you have found a new range extension if it is near the known range; or that you have found a snake captured by someone else and released outside its range, an unfortunate situation that occasionally, although infrequently, occurs. In either of these cases you should report your find to a nearby natural history museum, zoological garden, or university for verification.

Order

The order of appearance of the snakes in this book is phylogenetic—from the most primitive to the most advanced and in order of their relationships to one another—as we understand it now. Future studies, especially electrophoretic study of DNA, will probably result in some changes.

Names

Names used in this book come from a variety of sources. Many are from Collins' *Standard Common and Current Scientific Names for North American Amphibians and Reptiles,* third edition, 1990. Others are from Stebbins', *A Field Guide to Western Reptiles and Amphibians,* second edition, 1985. Others come from more recent literature, such as those for garter snakes, the rosy boa, and the red diamond rattlesnake. I have used those common names that I thought best described the species or that I felt were in most common usage regardless of "official" lists. In cases where more than one variation of a common name is widely used, the alternate is shown in parentheses.

A Spanish common name is given below the English name. Most of these come from Liner's *Scientific and Common Names for the Amphibians and Reptiles of Mexico in English and Spanish,* 1994.

This book identifies California's native snakes to species. Subspecies, where described, are listed at the end of each Species Account. "Subspecies," as used in this book, refers to geographical "races" in which color patterns, scale counts or arrangements, or other subtle differences in physiology or behavior set animals apart from others in the same species. This most often occurs in wide-ranging species, and particularly those populations made up of isolated *pockets* or ecological *islands* separated from each other by environmental barriers. These differences are often useful for identifying an animal by its location, or in studying the effects of isolation in the process of speciation. However, there is no general rule for what criteria are used to define a subspecies, and one man's subspecies may be another man's color variation and no more. Some authors prefer to use no subspecific taxa at all, while some books on snakes are arranged at the subspecies level. In this book I list many "recognized" subspecies, with the following understanding: Subspecies are not universally recognized by all authorities, and probably no two authors would cover this subject in exactly the same manner. Also, changes in classification occur continually as increased study allows for better understanding of the exact relationships of these animals to one another. For this reason subspecies come and go, although it is important to remember that the animals remain the same and it is only our knowledge of them that changes. Much of this knowledge is based on exciting new techniques for looking at genetics and DNA, but a lot of it is from good, old-fashioned observation such as that which eliminated subspecies of the longnose and common kingsnakes (see pages 86 and 79, respectively).

The point is, many subspecies are easily recognized and their characteristics are useful in identification, but the important unit of classification is the species. For example, it is more important to recognize an animal as a rosy boa than to determine whether it is a "coastal," "desert," "California," or other such designation. These categories are important to some field biologists and to herpetoculturists, but are not overly so to the person who only wants to know what a particular snake is. And a rosy boa by any other name is still a rosy boa.

I have chosen to include the citations of scientific names. The person's name that follows the species' (or subspecies') name in each account is that of the biologist who first described it and the date in which the original account was published. In cases where the name is still exactly the same as originally given, the authority's name appears without modification: for example, *Coluber constrictor* Linnaeus. If, however, changes have been made to the original name, the author's name will appear in parentheses, as in *Crotalus mitchelli* (Cope). Cope originally named the speckled rattlesnake *Caudisona mitchelli*.

The fact that changes have been made in light of more recent knowledge in no way detracts from Cope's original description, but the placing of his name in parentheses lets scholars know that changes have been made. This might not be of much interest to the general lay person who wants only to identify the snake he or she has just seen, but it is important to students of herpetology and to the historical understanding of the science, and I feel that it is too often left out of books of this kind.

Knowledge Yet To Be Gained

There are a lot of things we don't know about snakes, and it seems for every question answered two more occur. Are there new species to be discovered? It's not impossible, although California is pretty well explored. Still, there are some remote areas that have been less frequently explored by biologists, and new salamander and lizard species have been found in the past few decades. The Baja California rat snake, although an already described species, was not known to occur in California until the 1980s. A lot of range limits, habitat preferences, prey items, and other life history facts remain unknown, and a number of interesting behaviors have yet to be observed and recorded. As you learn to observe snakes in the wild, you may see something that no one else has seen before or recorded.

Keep a field notebook. Write down the date and location where you see a snake, and list other pertinent information—time, temperature, weather conditions, topography, vegetation, soil type, etc. Above all keep accurate notes of a snake's behavior. If you keep still after spotting a snake, especially if it hasn't detected your presence, you may have quite a period of time to observe it going about its daily life. Draw sketches, write down interesting actions. Your notes may one day be very important, but you can't rely on memory. As one zoology professor I know puts it, "If you didn't write it down, it did not happen."

VENOMOUS SNAKE IDENTIFICATION

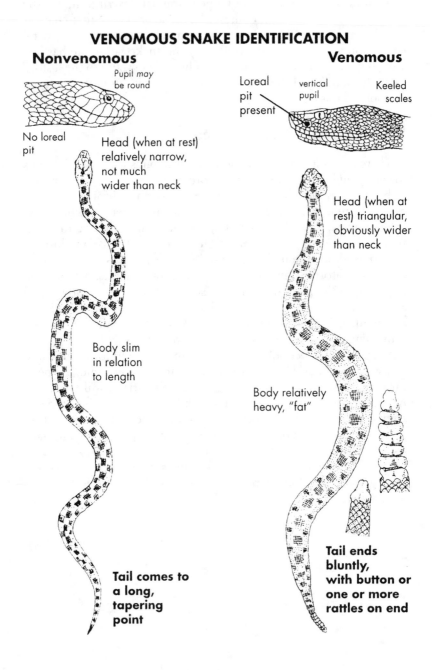

Nonvenomous

Pupil *may* be round

No loreal pit

Head (when at rest) relatively narrow, not much wider than neck

Body slim in relation to length

Tail comes to a long, tapering point

Venomous

Loreal pit present

vertical pupil

Keeled scales

Head (when at rest) triangular, obviously wider than neck

Body relatively heavy, "fat"

Tail ends bluntly, with button or one or more rattles on end

Venomous Snakes

Californians are relatively lucky in that we have representatives of only one group of dangerously venomous snakes within our borders. These are the rattlesnakes, genus *Crotalus,* of which we have six species in the state. Rattlesnakes possess one or more enlarged, hollow scales (the rattle) at the end of the tail, and have a number of other physical features that distinguish them from most of the non-venomous snakes in California (see page 8).

These characteristics are easily learned and observed. It is important to remember, however, that these "rules," while useful to know, have exceptions once you are outside California state lines. For instance, coral snakes (not found in California) do NOT have triangular heads, although they are highly venomous; and copperheads or water moccasins (not found in California) have tails that taper to a thin point, even though they are pit vipers as are rattlers.

Once you have learned to identify dangerous snakes, the next thing to learn is how to avoid coming into direct physical contact with them. This is actually a very simple process, and contains one cardinal rule: *Always watch where you put your hands and feet.* This rule means exactly what it says—if your hands and feet are always within your sight, anything that they might come in contact with is also in sight. You should never reach into holes or crevices with your hands, or under rocks and logs to turn them over. You never know what

might be under or in there, and snakes are not the only biting or sting-
ing creatures that inhabit such lairs. Nor should you reach up onto a
ledge that is above your line of sight. Such precipices are favorite sun-
ning places for snakes. Stick to paths when walking through tall grass
or scrub, and don't step over a log in the path, putting your foot out of
sight on the other side, however briefly. Step up on top of the log,
look at the other side, and step way out and over. If you know you're
going into an area inhabited by rattlesnakes, wear protective clothing
such as boots and loose-fitting, heavy jeans. Carry a walking stick to
beat the brush along the trailside, and look down as you walk along.

Accidents can still happen, of course. Although alert snakes will
leave an area if they feel threatened by a larger animal (including a
human), a cold or basking snake may be less responsive or may stay
inactive, in place, and must be approached closely before it reacts. A
rattlesnake will not always rattle for these reasons, although the purpose of the rattle appears to be as a warning for large animals to keep
their distance. Keep your eyes open as you traverse rattlesnake country.

Above all, use common sense. Remember that the people bitten
most often are those who are trying to catch or kill a rattlesnake,
tease it, or show off. And, statistically, it is young men between the
ages of 17 and 34, often under the influence of alcohol or "machis-
mo," who tempt fate. There is no reason to confront a rattlesnake
that is in the wild, and if you keep a minimum of a full body length
away from a snake, you are in no danger of being bitten. Even if a person is bitten by a rattler, there is no need to kill the snake to bring it
in for identification. Such an attempt only opens the possibility for
more bites, and it is not necessary. Since rattlers are the only dangerous snakes in California, no further identification is needed for treatment purposes. If a rattlesnake is encountered in an inhabited area,
authorities such as animal control, zoo, or herpetological society per-
sonnel should be contacted to remove it.

Another wise precaution is to hike or backpack with another person. This is sensible not only from the standpoint of possible
snakebite but also for any other emergency that might arise. If someone is hurt, ill, or bitten while away from "civilization," it is handy to
have someone else along who can go for help. A two-way radio or
cellular phone is also good to have in case of an emergency.

Recommended procedure (American Red Cross) for snakebite is
to *get to medical help as soon as possible.* This is not as difficult as it
might sound; I am often asked, "What if you are way out in the
wilderness, days from anywhere?" As a resident of overcrowded
southern California, it is hard for me to imagine such a scenario, but
I suppose it could still happen. In such cases, having a friend and
portable phone along will make all the difference between hours and
days of suffering, and further reinforces the need for them. Few

places are too far from helicopter or emergency vehicle access once the authorities have been contacted.

In case of a venomous snakebite, the companion should call 9-1-1 or the nearest hospital, and be prepared to give the victim's name, age, weight, height, any known allergies, and the details of the bite; he or she should then contact the nearest Poison Control Center and repeat the information, including to which hospital the victim is being taken. All possible efforts should be made to have the Poison Control authorities in direct contact with the hospital itself so that they can instruct the doctor. Most doctors have not had much training in snakebite treatment.

While waiting for medical help to arrive, other steps can be taken:

- Reassure the victim and keep him or her still.
- Set up for shock (lay the victim down with feet slightly elevated, cover with a blanket, jackets or other covering to prevent body heat loss), and force fluid.
- Remove watches, rings, bracelets, or other constricting items from the bitten appendage.
- Clean the bite area.
- Maintain an airway and be prepared to administer mouth-to-mouth resuscitation or CPR, if you have had training for it (a good idea for everyone at any rate).
- Immobilize the site.

DO NOT:

- Give the victim alcoholic beverages or tobacco products.
- Give the victim morphine or other central nervous system depressors.
- Make any deep cuts at the bite site. Doing this opens capillaries that provide a direct route for venom into the blood stream.
- Pack ice or cold packs directly onto the site; frostbite is as damaging as snakebite!
- Use a tourniquet or other restrictive device.
- Break open large blisters that form around the bite site.

Suction is of little value, but may be employed if one is using the Extractor®, a type of suction device that is available at sporting goods and outdoor equipment stores. Little rubber suction cups (the traditional snakebite kit) have little or no drawing power and are essentially useless. The Extractor® is effective if used immediately, and if you have one, use it. Don't use your mouth to perform suction except as a last resort; if you have any cuts or open sores (or cavities) in your mouth, you could suffer from poisoning as well. Suction will remove up to 30% of the venom within the first 30 minutes, but is usually ineffective beyond that length of time.

Death from snakebite is extremely rare in California. Most fairly healthy adult people are large enough to absorb a snakebite without fatal effects, and the venoms of most of our rattlers are not deadly to large animals. However, snakebite is dangerous due to the composition of the venom and its actions on tissues. Snake venom has evolved as a means for the snake to procure food. The bite is not only meant to kill prey, but to start the process of digestion by breaking down tissues. The components of most rattlesnake venoms are *hemotoxic,* that is, tissue destructive; they affect the circulatory system, destroying blood cells, damaging skin tissues, and causing internal hemorrhaging. In addition, there are varying amounts of *neurotoxic,* or nerve-affecting, compounds. These immobilize the nerve system, making the victim's breathing difficult or stopping it completely. Generally, rattlesnake venoms are dominated by hemotoxic properties, while those of the sea snake, coral snake and cobra groups (hydrophiids and elapids) are dominated by neurotoxins. A notable exception to this is in young rattlesnakes and in the Mojave rattlesnake, in which neurotoxic components predominate. But all snake venoms contain a mixture of properties that affect their victims in various ways.

Another statistic worth knowing is that 25% or more of bites by adult rattlesnakes on humans are "dry" bites—the rattler did not inject any venom, only biting the victim out of fear or alarm. The pain from a rattlesnake bite typically occurs soon after the incident. This is usually followed by rapid swelling around the site. If these symptoms do not appear within minutes, chances are it was a dry bite. Again, however, this may not be true in the case of bites by baby rattlers or by the Mojave rattlesnake. Juvenile rattlesnake venoms contain fewer lytic (tissue-decomposing) enzymes and have relatively higher concentrations of neurotoxins, particularly cardiotoxic compounds, than do adult snakes. The Mojave rattlesnake is so extremely dangerous because it is a large snake with retained "juvenile" venom characteristics (Sweet, 1997).

Many snakes will bite, of course, especially in self-defense, but bites from any of our nonvenomous species are relatively minor. The area should be cleansed and dressed with an antiseptic and bandage, if necessary. Generally no further treatment is necessary.

Finally, remember that freshly-killed snakes have nervous systems that may still be active, and a dead snake may still deliver a bite. Do not attempt to handle a venomous snake, even if you think it is dead. There is an old folk saying that if you kill a snake it will not die until sundown. While there is no specific time that a snake breathes its last, the folklore simply points out the known fact that snakes can still move and react, sometimes for hours, after they are fatally injured.

Precaution and common sense will allow you to safely enjoy viewing all of our native snakes, including the rattlers, valuable and fascinating in their own right.

SCALES OF A SNAKE'S HEAD

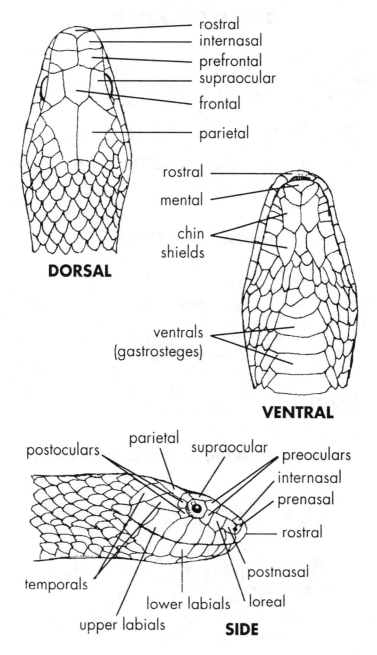

rostral
internasal
prefrontal
supraocular
frontal
parietal

DORSAL

rostral
mental
chin
shields

ventrals
(gastrosteges)

VENTRAL

postoculars   parietal   supraocular   preoculars
internasal
prenasal
rostral
temporals
postnasal
lower labials   loreal
upper labials   **SIDE**

DORSAL SCALE TYPES

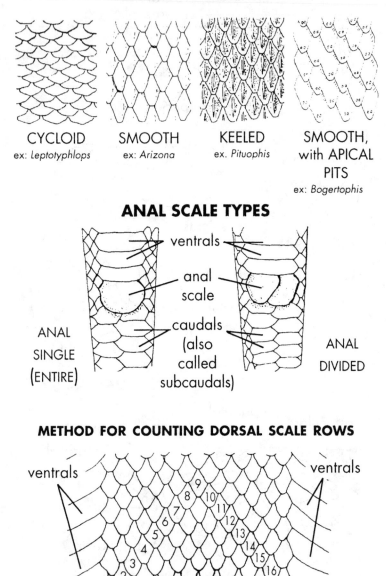

CYCLOID
ex: *Leptotyphlops*

SMOOTH
ex: *Arizona*

KEELED
ex. *Pituophis*

SMOOTH,
with APICAL
PITS
ex: *Bogertophis*

ANAL SCALE TYPES

ventrals

anal
scale

caudals
(also
called
subcaudals)

ANAL
SINGLE
(ENTIRE)

ANAL
DIVIDED

METHOD FOR COUNTING DORSAL SCALE ROWS

ventrals

ventrals

Identification

"A bird in the hand is worth two in the bush."

When you see a snake, often it will be for just a brief moment. Practice looking for its most observable features—colors, stripes, general shape, etc. Many of these will be the characteristics that identify a particular species. Look at the photos in the color section to see if you can find a close match, then turn to the Species Account for the most likely possibility. The range map, detailed description, and illustrations should either confirm your deductions or lead you to look again (a "similar species" section in some Species Accounts helps with this).

With diligence and a little practice, almost anyone can learn to identify most of California's snakes by sight. After all, most of us know birders who can accurately ID a bird at the merest glance because they are thoroughly familiar with the characteristic markings for each species. With only 38 species of snakes compared to the hundreds of birds that live in or pass through California, your job is infinitely easier. Old adages aside, it is much easier to get a snake in the hand, and doing so is sometimes necessary for absolute identification.

The positive identification of some snakes may require examination of scales, particularly those of the head, midbody, and tail. Many of these scales are named, as shown on pages 13 and 14, and it is worth taking the time to learn them to make the use of this guide faster and more convenient. It is the arrangement, shape, and pattern of these scales that you use to identify a snake using a "key" (see pages 18–29).

Don't let the technical sound of the scale names deter you from learning them. They are quite easy, actually. Certain prefixes denote position: *pre* (in front of); *post* (behind); *sub* (below); *supra* (above). Other names connote body parts: *rostrum* (snout); *nasal* (nose, nostrils); *ocular* (eye); *labium* (lip); and so on. So a *preocular* scale is in front of the eye. A *postnasal* scale is behind the scale that has the nostril in it. And the *labials* are the lip scales—upper labials on the upper jaw and lower labials on the lower jaw.

Dorsum refers to the upper surface of an animal, so the dorsal coloration of a snake means the color of its back. The *venter,* or *ventral,* surface is the underside, the belly. *Lateral* refers to the sides, *dorsolateral* to the upper sides. *Caudal* is tail, and *subcaudal* scales are those on the underside of the tail. *Anterior* is toward the front of, and *posterior is toward the rear of;* proximal is nearest, *distal* is farthest away. Etymologies (derivative sources) of scientific names are given in the text for some of the snakes.

Scales may also have to be counted on the body. This is usually done at midbody, and scales are counted diagonally from the edge of one ventral to the mid-dorsal line, then down the other side to the edge of the ventral on the opposite side. This is referred to as the *scale row* count in the Keys and the Species Accounts. Scale rows are also occasionally counted on the anterior part of the body (the neck) and on the tail just before the vent. Some references list these as a scale formula, for example, 15-17-13 being scale row counts from front to back. Normally the midbody scale row counts will suffice.

Capture of Snakes for Identification

As previously mentioned, it is often desirous to have the snake in hand for identification. Many snakes can simply be picked up, and neither special techniques nor equipment is needed. However, many will bite, and a few will spread fecal matter or foul-smelling musk over their captors. For these reasons gloves and a snake stick (see below) may be handy. Obviously, venomous species should never be handled—rely upon range maps and descriptions for these. Fortunately, California's venomous snakes are easily recognized and are best left alone (see Venomous Snakes chapter). However, should you come across a roadkill or otherwise dead venomous snake, this will allow you an opportunity to observe its scalation up close. A word of warning: A dead rattlesnake can still bite! Snakes have reflexes that keep them moving, in some cases for hours after an injury that kills them. Approach a dead snake carefully, use a snake stick to pin the head down and observe it that way. Do not attempt to handle it.

A *snake stick* is merely a three- to four-foot pole with a 90-degree angle iron attached to one end. This can easily be made with a broom stick or piece of doweling. The "hook" on the end can be used to slip underneath a snake and lift it, or it can be used to pin down its body or head in order for you to get a hand on it without being bitten. Once you have used one of these you will see how the proverbial "forked stick" would be a most inadequate, possibly harmful tool.

Keep in mind that in the case of endangered species, sight identification will have to do. This is because it is illegal to capture or attempt to capture or otherwise "harass" endangered species. Also, remember that to take or possess reptiles in California (this includes catching them just for identification purposes), you must be at least 16 years old and have a valid California Sport Fishing License (see Conservation and the Law chapter). In all cases, reptiles that can be captured should be handled carefully so as not to injure or unduly stress them and, after examination and identification, released where caught.

Keys to the Snakes of California

With snake firmly in hand (generally held securely behind the head while supporting the rest of the body), it is time to look closely at its scales and "key it out." The key is a device in which you are given choices to make based upon your observation of the specimen at (or in) hand. This is a typical *dichotomous* key, meaning two-branched. Each set of queries is in couplets, and both should be read completely before a choice is made. Whichever choice is most like the specimen will lead to the next set of choices, and so on. This is generally a fairly easy process and will take you in the right direction immediately. If, at the end, your specimen does not key out correctly, go back and start again. Some snakes appear in the key more than once, because there is more than one possible path to reach them. For example, the lyre snake may have a single or divided anal plate, and the spotted leafnose snake usually has smooth scales, but they may be keeled in males. Don't be discouraged—with practice, this will become second nature. Once you have keyed out your specimen, check the Species Accounts for further details of identification.

I. Key to the Genera of California Snakes

Numbers in parentheses following a snake's name indicate the number of the Species Account.

1a. No enlarged ventral scales; scales uniform all the way around body 2

1b. Ventral plates present (enlarged transverse scales on belly); eyes well-developed 3

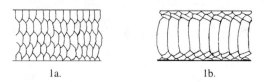

1a.   1b.

2a. Wormlike snake with eyes concealed beneath ocular scales, tail extremely short with sharp spine at tip ....
................................Western blind snake *Leptotyphlops humilis* (1)

2b. Ocean-dwelling snake; eyes distinct and nostrils high on snout; flattened, oarlike tail ....
.... Yellowbelly sea snake *Pelamis platurus* (32)

3a. No loreal pit on side of face between eye and nostril; no rattle at end of tail 4

3b. Loreal pit present; rattle at end of tail ....
.... Rattlesnakes, genus *Crotalus* (33–38)
(see Key II)

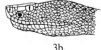

3a.   3b.

4a. No elongated paired chin shields between lower labials 5

4b. Two pairs (rarely one pair) of well-defined chin shields between lower labials 6

4a.   4b.

5a. Scales on top of head small...
.... Rosy boa *Lichanura trivirgata* (3)
5b. Scales on top of head enlarged...
.... Rubber boa *Charina bottae* (2)
6a. Dorsal scales keeled, sometimes only faintly on the uppermost
scale rows and on the posterior part of the body 7
6b. Dorsal scales smooth 9

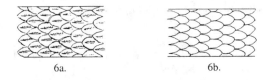

6a.   6b.

7a. Twenty-seven or more scale rows; prefrontals usually four............
.... Gopher snake *Pituophis catenifer* (14)
7b. Less than 27 scale rows; prefrontals two 8

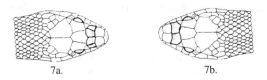

7a.   7b.

8a. Pupil round; no suboculars; rostral not enlarged or with free lateral edges; eight or more lower labials ....
.... Garter snakes, genus *Thamnophis* (18–25)
(see Key VI)
8b. Pupil elliptical; suboculars present; rostral very large with free lateral edges.... Spotted leafnose snake *Phyllorhynchus decurtatus* (6)

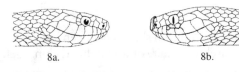

8a.   8b.

9a. Anal plate single.. 10
9b. Anal plate divided.. 14

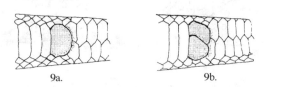

9a.   9b.

10a. All or most caudals divided 11
10b. Most caudals entire ..... Longnose snake *Rhinocheilus lecontei* (17)

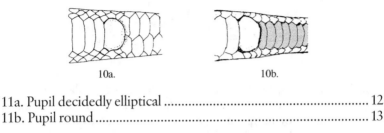

10a.   10b.

11a. Pupil decidedly elliptical 12
11b. Pupil round 13

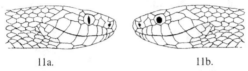

11a.   11b.

12a. Suboculars present ....
.... Spotted leafnose snake *Phyllorhynchus decurtatus* (6)
12b. No suboculars (upper labials in contact with the eye) ....
.... Lyre snake *Trimorphodon biscutatus* (30)

12a.   12b.

13a. Ventral surface light-colored, without dark markings ....
.... Glossy snake *Arizona elegans* (13)
13b. Ventral surface with at least some dark markings ....
.... Kingsnakes, genus *Lampropeltis* (15–16)
(see Key III)
14a. Fewer than 19 scale rows 15
14b. Nineteen or more scale rows.. 24
15a. Rostral not enlarged, lateral edges not free 16
15b. Rostral much enlarged, with free lateral edges* ....
......................Western patchnose snake *Salvadora hexalepis* (11)
16a. Loreal present.. 17
16b. No loreal... 23

16a.   16b.

---

*The scales are keeled in the lateral rows above the anal region in mature males, but the genus
is placed under "smooth scales" in Key.

17a. Two or 3 preoculars 18
17b. Usually 1 preocular 21

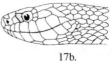

17a.   17b.

18a. Anterior temporals usually 2 or 3; lower preocular very small, wedged between adjacent upper labials 19
18b. One anterior temporal; lower preocular not wedged between upper labials 20

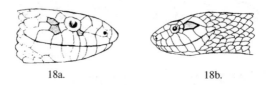

18a.   18b.

19a. Fifteen scale rows at posterior end of body ....
.... Racer *Coluber constrictor* (7)
19b. Scale rows at posterior end of body 13, 12, or 11 .....Coachwhip, Striped racer, and Whipsnakes, genus *Masticophis* (8–10)
(see Key IV)
20a. Nasal plate divided; ring on neck or black spots on belly or both
.... Ringneck snake *Diadophis punctatus* (4)
20b. Nasal plate entire 21

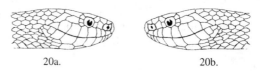

20a.   20b.

21a. Ventral surface with uniform light color or, if dark markings are present, they are black rings that encircle the body; no lateral light stripe on the fourth or fifth scale rows 22
21b. Each ventral scale with a dark anterior border; usually a light stripe on the fourth or fifth row of scales ....
.... Sharptail snake *Contia tenuis* (5)

22a. Nasal valve usually prominent; abdomen angled; snout flattened, spade-like .... Western shovelnose snake *Chionactis occipitalis* (27)

22b. Nasal valve less developed; abdomen rounded; snout rounded in profile .... Ground snake *Sonora semiannulata* (26)

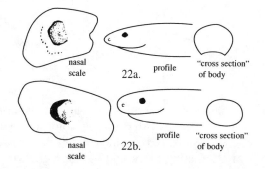

nasal scale   22a.   profile   "cross section" of body

nasal scale   22b.   profile   "cross section" of body

23a. Fifteen scale rows; snout flattened, shovel-like............................ .... Western shovelnose snake *Chionactis occipitalis* (27)

23b. Snout not flattened or shovel-like; coloration above uniform except near head ... Black-headed snakes, genus *Tantilla* (28–29) (see Key V)

24a. Pupil round ..... Baja California rat snake *Bogertophis rosaliae* (12)

24b. Pupil elliptical 25

25a. Usually one loreal; 2 postoculars; 1 anterior temporal; 7 or 8 upper labials .... Night snake *Hypsiglena torquata* (31)

25b. Two or more loreals; 3 or 4 postoculars; 2 or 3 anterior temporals; usually 9 or more upper labials .... Lyre snake *Trimorphodon biscutatus* (30)

II. Key to the Species of Rattlesnakes, Genus *Crotalus*

26a. Outer edges of supraoculars extended into raised and flexible, hornlike projections, pointed at the tip .... Sidewinder *Crotalus cerastes* (36)

26b. Outer edges of supraoculars not extended into raised and flexible projections 27

26a.   26b.

27a. Prenasals in contact with rostral; upper preocular not divided, or if divided, loreal conspicuously longer than high............... 28

27b. Prenasals usually separated from rostral by small scales or granules; upper preoculars often divided horizontally, vertically, or both .... Speckled (Southwestern speckled) rattlesnake
Crotalus mitchelli pyrrhus (35)

27a.   27b.

28a. Tail of alternating black and light ash-gray rings, both colors in sharp contrast with the posterior body color which may be gray, dark gray, cream, pink, red, red-brown, or olive-brown 29

28b. Tail not of alternating black and light ash-gray rings in strong color contrast to posterior body color.................................. 31

28a.   28b.

29a. Dark and light tail rings of approximately equal width; postocular light stripe, if present, intersects upper labials 1 to 3 scales in front of the angle of the mouth; minimum number of scales between supraoculars 3 or more; no definite line of demarcation between scales in the frontal and prefrontal areas; proximal (base) rattle black 30

29b. Dark tail rings narrower than light ones; postocular light stripe, if present, passes backward above the angle of the mouth; minimum number of scales between supraoculars rarely more than 2 (see Figure 31a); definite division line or suture between scales in frontal and prefrontal areas; lower half of proximal rattle light in color .... Mojave rattlesnake *Crotalus scutulatus* (38)

29a.   29b.

30a. First lower labials usually not divided transversely; general color cream, buff, gray, or gray-brown; dark punctuations are conspicuous in the markings ....
.................Western diamondback rattlesnake *Crotalus atrox* (33)

30b. First lower labials usually divided transversely; general color pink, red, brick-red, or red-brown; dark punctuations weakly in evidence or absent from markings ....
.... Red diamond rattlesnake *Crotalus exsul* (34)

30a.   30b.

31a. Two internasals 32

31b. More than two internasals in contact with rostral, regardless of size or position.............Western rattlesnake *Crotalus viridis* (37)

31a.   32b.

32a. Supraoculars pitted, sutured, or with outer edges broken ....
.... Speckled (Panamint) rattlesnake *Crotalus mitchelli stephensi* (35)

32b. Supraoculars not pitted, sutured, or with broken outer edges; dorsal pattern consists of single row of dark blotches; usually 1 loreal; tail rings sharply contrasting in color ....
.... Mojave rattlesnake *Crotalus scutulatus* (38)

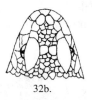

32a.   32b.

III. Key to the Species of Kingsnakes, Genus *Lampropeltis*

33a. Pattern of rings or crossbands including red, bordered by black...
.............California mountain kingsnake *Lampropeltis zonata* (16)
33b. Pattern of rings, crossbands, or stripes; light rings much wider on lower rows of scales than they are at the middorsal line; no red in pattern ....Common kingsnake *Lampropeltis getula* (15)

33a.   33b.

IV. Key to the Species of Racers, Whipsnakes, and Coachwhips, Genus *Masticophis*

34a. Scales in 15 rows at midbody...
.... Striped whipsnake *Masticophis taeniatus* (10)
34b. Scales in 17 rows at midbody...35
35a. Distinct longitudinal lateral stripes present, one on each side, extending onto tail............Striped racer *Masticophis lateralis* (9)
35b. Without distinct longitudinal stripes.......................................
....Coachwhip *Masticophis flagellum* (8)

V. Key to the Species of Black-headed Snakes, Genus *Tantilla*

36a. Black on head extends below angle of mouth and into gular scales ....Western black-headed snake *Tantilla planiceps* (28)
36b. Black on head not extending below angle of the mouth into gular scales ....
..... Southwestern black-headed snake *Tantilla hobartsmithi* (29)

36a.   36b.

VI. Key to the Species of Garter Snakes, Genus *Thamnophis*

Note: The garter snakes are a taxonomist's nightmare, or perhaps dream group, depending upon his or her aspirations. They have received much attention throughout the years and still remain a confusing group. Many of the Western species have been repeatedly reclassified as herpetologists strove to make sense of the group. For instance, the two-striped garter snake, *Thamnophis hammondii*, was previously known as *T. couchii hammondii*, and before that *T. elegans hammondii*. The western aquatic garter snake, *T. atratus*, has in the past been known as *T. elegans atratus* and *T. ordinoides atratus*. While much progress has been made in sorting out these snakes, there is always a need for further study.

This key is very general, and due to the great variation (even within a given species) and the fact that some species look remarkably like others, you may have to rely on range maps and other information in the illustrations to help identify a specimen of *Thamnophis*. A very detailed key (to all garter snakes) can be found in Rossman, Ford, and Seigel's *The Garter Snakes, Evolution and Ecology* (1996).

37a. Lateral stripes anteriorly on third row of scales only; light-colored crescents present behind the mouth.....................................
.... Checkered garter snake *Thamnophis marcianus* (25)
37b. Lateral stripes anteriorly on scales of the second and third rows... 38

37a.   37b.

38a. Seven upper labials 39
38b. Eight upper labials 41
39a. Ventrals less than 153; dorsal stripe red or yellow; dorsal scales in 19 rows (occasionally 17) at midbody; pale yellowish flecks between scales in areas between stripes ....
.... Northwestern garter snake *Thamnophis ordinoides* (24)
39b. Ventrals more than 153; dorsal stripe bright yellow; no pale flecking in area between stripes; posterior chin shields markedly longer than anterior pair..40
40a. Ground color sufficiently dark to obscure dorsal spots; top of head mainly black ....
.... Common (Valley) garter snake *Thamnophis sirtalis fitchi* (18)

40b. Ground color paler, not entirely obscuring dorsal stripes; top of head olive or reddish; stripes narrow and bright yellow..............
.... Common garter snake *Thamnophis sirtalis* (18)
41a. Dorsal stripe bright yellow and well-developed...................... 42
41b. Dorsal stripe faint, discontinuous, or absent............................ 44
42a. Two preoculars on one or both sides of the head; scale rows 21, 22, or 23 at a point ⅓ of the distance between the head and the vent; middorsal stripe involving one and two half-scale rows ....
....................................Western terrestrial (Klamath) garter snake
Thamnophis elegans biscutatus (19)
42b. One preocular; scale rows 19, 20, or 21 when counted ⅓ of the distance between the head and the vent.................................. 43

42a.   42b.

43a. Red markings often present on sides or on ventral surface; lateral stripes sometimes red; head narrow; ventrals usually fewer than 160..
...............Western aquatic garter snake *Thamnophis atratus* (20)
43b. No red in coloration; head wide, somewhat swollen; ventrals usually more than 160; 21 (occasionally 20 or 19) scale rows; ground color of dorsolateral area nearly black—sufficiently dark as to almost obscure superimposed dark spots; posterior chin shields not much longer than anterior............ Western terrestrial (mountain) garter snake *Thamnophis elegans elegans* (19)
44a. Dorsal stripe absent; lateral stripe usually well-developed; dorsal spots small and inconspicuous..
.... Two-striped garter snake *Thamnophis hammondii* (23)
44b. Dorsal stripe present, but faint or confined to the anterior part of the body 45
45a. Dorsal stripe visible for full length of body but faint or irregular 46
45b. Dorsal stripe faint, usually confined to the anterior part of the body; dorsal surfaces checkered with large, squarish blotches; iris uniformly brown or gray.. 47
46a. Scales in 21 rows; faint, irregular dorsal stripe, which may be invaded by small, rounded dorsal spots; iris dark brown with a yellow rim around pupil.............. Western terrestrial (wandering) garter snake *Thamnophis elegans vagrans* (19)

46b. Scale rows usually 23; dorsal stripe dull yellow, faint, but present for much of the length; head brown with no contrasting facial markings; length often more than 700 mm ..... Giant garter snake *Thamnophis gigas* (22)

47a. Twenty-one scale rows in both neck region and midbody; dorsal stripe often confined to neck region ....
.... Sierra garter snake *Thamnophis couchii* (21)

47b. Nineteen scale rows either in neck region or at midbody or both; dorsal stripe discernible at least on anterior half of body ....
.... Western aquatic (Oregon) garter snake *Thamnophis atratus hydrophilus* (20)

SPECIES ACCOUNTS

Family
Leptotyphlopidae:
Slender Blind Snakes

Slender blind snakes are considered primitive, that is, closer to their evolutionary ancestors in form and function than more "advanced" snakes. One of their primitive traits is possession of a fairly well-developed pelvic girdle and rudimentary femurs (thigh bones) that manifest as anal spurs, particularly in females. These spurs are internal, but rarely may protrude through pores just behind the snake's anal opening (Shaw and Campbell, 1974). Another curious feature of their anatomy is that they have teeth only in the lower jaw.

Because of their resemblance to earthworms, these snakes are sometimes called worm snakes. They are also known as thread snakes in the Old World. They are usually under 18 in. (45 cm) in length and are brown, purplish, gray, or pink with a lighter underside. The body is slender and cylindrical, and the head is continuous with the body (no neck constriction). The scales are smooth, shiny, uniform in size, and completely encircle the body—there are no enlarged ventral scales. California's native species has a sharp spine at the end of the tail. The eyes are vestigial, appearing as dark spots beneath the ocular scales; they are truly blind, although probably capable of distinguishing light and dark. The slender form, uniform scales, and degenerate eyes distinguish them from all other California snakes. Generally, the only other reptile they can be confused with is the California legless lizard, *Anniella pulchra*. This unusual reptile is shiny silver or black above, often yellow below. It has moveable eyelids and is capable of losing its tail for escape from predation.

Blind snakes are crevice dwellers and burrowers. They live in loose soil, sand, humus, or leaf litter and come to the surface only at night or on overcast days. They generally live in damp situations, as they appear especially susceptible to desiccation. The solidly constructed skull, slender form, and smooth scales allow them to easily penetrate the ant and termite nests in which they find food. They subsist on ants, ant eggs, larvae and pupae, and termites.

The genus *Leptotyphlops* contains around 75 species in North America, South America, the West Indies, tropical Africa, and southwestern Asia. One species occurs in California.

1 Western Blind Snake

Culebrilla Ciega de Occidente

Leptotyphlops humilis (Baird & Girard, 1853)

Leptos, Greek = slender; *typhos,* Greek = blind; *ops,* Greek = eye; *humilis,* Latin = small or ground-dwelling

Habitat   This snake is found in habitats ranging from deserts to inland valleys where there is suitable loose substrate for burrowing. It often inhabits hillsides with rocky outcrops and

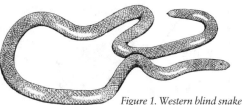

Figure 1. Western blind snake

loose soil, frequently found in canyons where small streams are present. It seems to prefer areas in which some moisture is present, although it does not seem to be restricted to such areas. However, it is generally absent from situations such as dry lake bottoms, alluvial fans, or sandy flats, which have virtually no moisture. It burrows around the roots of plants and beneath rocks or other surface objects, and in ant and termite nests.

Prey   This snake preys on ants, ant pupae, ant larvae, termites, other small insects and their larvae, spiders, millipedes, and centipedes. Its cylindrical shape and solid head adapt it to entering nests of these creatures and preying upon them. They prefer to eat eggs and pupae, but will eat adult workers (they avoid the soldiers), although the snake may try to break the heads off the adult insects before swallowing them.

Behavior   Though it is probably quite common, this snake is rarely seen. It occasionally comes to the surface at night and can sometimes be found by night driving. Even then, its small size and slender form are easily overlooked. By day it can occasionally be encountered by looking into rock crevices or searching under flat rocks or other surface objects in areas of loose soil.

When disturbed, this snake will empty its cloaca and smear its tormentor with the foul-smelling contents. It also smears itself with the same substance—making it unpalatable to other, ophiophagous (snake-eating) snakes and also repelling ants and termites whose nest it may be entering. In addition, when following ant trails these snakes pick up the scent of the ants, which repels many enemies as well.

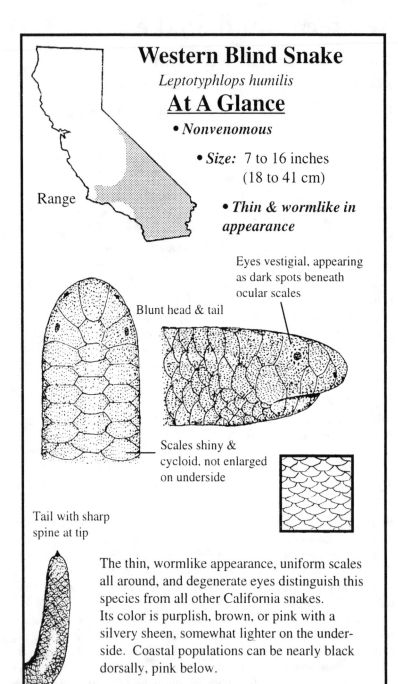

Western Blind Snake
Leptotyphlops humilis
At A Glance
- *Nonvenomous*

  - *Size:* 7 to 16 inches
    (18 to 41 cm)

    - *Thin & wormlike in appearance*

Range

Eyes vestigial, appearing as dark spots beneath ocular scales

Blunt head & tail

Scales shiny & cycloid, not enlarged on underside

Tail with sharp spine at tip

The thin, wormlike appearance, uniform scales all around, and degenerate eyes distinguish this species from all other California snakes.
Its color is purplish, brown, or pink with a silvery sheen, somewhat lighter on the under-side. Coastal populations can be nearly black dorsally, pink below.

This snake uses the sharp tip of the tail to anchor itself in a burrow so it can thrust the rest of its body forward. On the surface, it will probe with this spine thrusting it into the ground to propel itself ahead. To a person unexpecting of such behavior who picks this snake up, it might appear as though the snake is trying to "sting" the hand that holds it. No snake possesses a sting of any kind, at either the front or back end.

The Western blind snake is capable of burrowing with considerable speed into loose soil. This snake seems to be most active between April and August.

Reproduction The blind snake is an egg layer. Two to 6 (average 4) eggs, measuring approximately 5 by 15 mm, are laid in July or August. The adult female may coil about the eggs, much as some pythons do, perhaps to help prevent their desiccation (drying out). The eggs hatch in one or two months, neonates (newly hatched young) being about 3 inches (7.5 cm) long.

Similar Species Because of its combination of unique characteristics, this snake can be confused with no other species in California.

Notes A scientist collecting scorpions in Arizona made a startling discovery about this snake. Scorpions shine an eerie pale green in the beam of a fluorescent "black light," and scientists utilize these lights to locate scorpions at night. It was discovered that the Western blind snake, too, fluoresces—its rostral scales are bright blue while the rest of the body glows a pale green.

Subspecies Two subspecies are recognized in California.

Desert Blind Snake

Leptotyphlops humilis cahuilae Klauber, 1931

(named for Lake Cahuila, near the area it was first found)

Distinguishing Characteristics This subspecies has five lightly pigmented dorsal scale rows. There are usually 285 or more dorsal scales.

Notes This desert dweller is associated with smoke tree (*Dalea spinosa*), desert willow (*Chilopsis linearis*), brittle bush (*Encelia farinosa*), and ocotillo (*Fouquieria splendens*)—typical plants of low desert canyons and sandy washes. This is one of the largest snakes in the genus *Leptotyphlops*, with a maximum recorded length of 389 mm.

Southwestern Blind Snake

Leptotyphlops humilis humilis (Baird & Girard, 1853)

Distinguishing Characteristics   This subspecies has twelve scale rows around the body at the tail. The fourth middorsal scale is undivided, and the fifth dorsal scale is not much, if any, wider than the sixth. There are seven or more heavily pigmented dorsal scale rows, and usually fewer than 285 dorsals.

Notes   This subspecies is associated with the Upper Sonoran life zone in association with such plants as white sage (*Salvia apiana*), buckwheat (*Eriogonum* sp.), chamise (*Adenostoma fasciculatum*), scrub oak (*Quercus dumosa*), and holly-leafed cherry (*Prunus ilicifolia*)–plants typical of chaparral or brushy hillsides.

Family Boidae: Boas

BOAS

The boa family comprises 39 species in 12 genera found in both the Old and New Worlds, including temperate western North America. It contains one of the world's largest serpents (the green anaconda, *Eunectes murinus*) as well as many smaller forms. Generally, these are heavy-bodied animals with smooth, often glossy scales and vertical eye pupils, although many smaller boas are slender with very long tails (such as tree boas, *Corallus* sp.). Vestiges of hind limbs are present, particularly in males, in the form of tiny "spurs" on each side of the vent. Most species have temperature-sensitive pits on the labial (lip) scales that help them locate warm-blooded prey. Prey is killed by constriction.

Boas are considered primitive snakes because, like the slender blind snakes, they have the vestiges of a pelvic girdle and anal spurs which are rudimentary hind limbs. These are external and noticeable on many boa and python species and are usually larger in males. These spurs are attached to muscles and can be moved. The males use these spurs in courtship and copulation to stimulate the female snake. Unlike most snakes, boas have two functional lungs, the right being larger than the left.

Boas are ovoviviparous: the eggs are hatched within the body of the female and the young are born live.

Two boa species occur in California.

2 Rubber Boa

Boa de Goma Elástica

Charina bottae (Blainville, 1835)

Charina, Greek = graceful; *bottae*, honoring Paolo Emilio Botta, a 19th-Century explorer, archaeologist, and diplomat who collected the type (originally described) specimen

Habitat   While the rubber boa has a large geographic range (besides the range it occupies in California it also extends northward into British Columbia and eastward to southern Utah and central Wyoming), its distribution is actually spotty due to its environmental needs. This snake is found in grassland and woodland areas, chaparral, and forests—a wide array of habitat types from sea level to 10,000 feet in elevation and nearly always in the vicinity of water. It is usually found beneath rotting logs, under the bark of fallen or standing dead trees, or under rocks. It is both a good swimmer and a good climber, but it is a superb burrower and spends much of its time underground.

Prey   The rubber boa eats small mammals (especially young mice and shrews), birds, lizards, insects, salamanders, and other snakes. Prey is killed by constriction.

Behavior   This snake is largely crepuscular to nocturnal in habits, although occasionally it may be encountered during the day. This is especially true on cool, overcast days, although they have been observed basking in the sunlight on occasion. When alarmed, it will roll itself into a ball, concealing its head among the coils, and feigning head-like motions (even "striking") with its blunt tail. This has earned it the nickname "two-headed" snake. It also seems to use the tail to fend off adult mice while it is feeding upon the young in their nest, and it is not unusual for an adult rubber boa to have heavy scarring on the tail.

Reproduction   Rubber boas are live-bearing, with 2 to 8 young born between August and November. Young are about 8 inches long.

Similar Species   This snake cannot be confused with any other species within its range. The only other California boa, the rosy boa (3), lacks large scales on the top of the head, and their ranges do not overlap.

Notes   Rubber boas are more tolerant of cold conditions than most other serpents and have even reported to have escaped into

Rubber Boa
Charina bottae
At A Glance
• *Nonvenomous*

• *Size:* 14 to 33 inches (35 to 83 cm)

• *Stocky and "rubbery" in appearance*

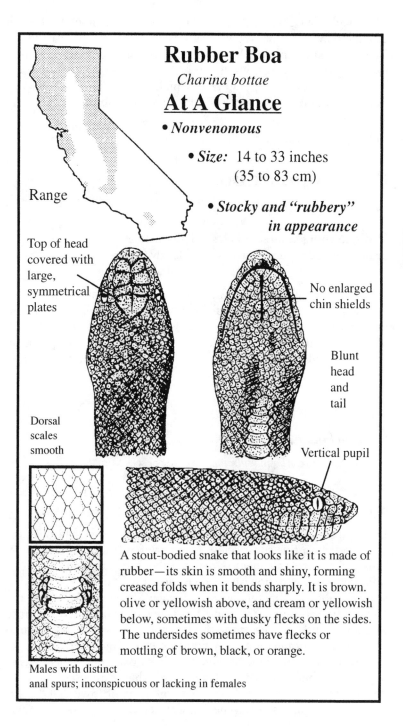

Range

Top of head covered with large, symmetrical plates

No enlarged chin shields

Blunt head and tail

Dorsal scales smooth

Vertical pupil

Males with distinct anal spurs; inconspicuous or lacking in females

A stout-bodied snake that looks like it is made of rubber—its skin is smooth and shiny, forming creased folds when it bends sharply. It is brown. olive or yellowish above, and cream or yellowish below, sometimes with dusky flecks on the sides. The undersides sometimes have flecks or mottling of brown, black, or orange.

snow banks (Wright and Wright, 1957; Shaw and Campbell, 1974). In general, they are active at temperatures between 59° to 76°F (15° to 24°C), considerably cooler than the optimum temperatures preferred by other snakes. Predictably, they also have a lower critical high temperature (temperature at which locomotion becomes disabled) than other snakes—at 100.4°F (Shaw and Campbell, 1974).

Subspecies   Three subspecies of Rubber Boa have been described, all found in California:

Pacific Rubber Boa

Charina bottae bottae (Blainville, 1835)

Distinguishing Characteristics   This snake has 45 or more lengthwise scale rows at midbody (not counting the ventrals). The parietal scale is usually divided.

Notes   Although there is a difference in the scale counts and the division of the parietal scale, many authorities believe there are no differences major enough to recognize the subspecies *C. b. utahensis* as separate from this one. Specimens from areas of probable intergradation (such as northeastern California) should be looked at carefully to help clarify this situation.

Southern Rubber Boa

Charina bottae umbratica Klauber, 1943

umbratica, from the Latin *umbraticus* = shade or seclusion

Status   This subspecies is listed as **THREATENED** by the state and is protected.

Distinguishing Characteristics   Scale rows are usually 44 or fewer at midbody on this subspecies. There are fewer than 192 ventrals. This snake is often smaller in size than other subspecies and frequently lighter in color—yellowish, "camel" tan, or light olive. It is found in scattered localities in southern California: Mt. Pinos, Mt. Abel, the Tehachapi, San Bernardino, and San Jacinto Mountains. This snake is found at fairly high elevations and, in some cases, is widely separated from other populations. Raymond Cowles suggested that it might also be found on Big Pine Mountain in Santa Barbara County (McKeown, 1997), but this area has been thoroughly searched and no evidence of their existence there has come to light (Sweet, 1997). It appears to be missing from the San Gabriel Mountains of Los Angeles County, a logical link between known populations. If it is to be found there (and this area, too, has been thoroughly searched), it will probably be in the yellow pine forest community as it is in the nearby San Bernardino and San Jacinto Mountains (Schoenherr, 1976).

Notes   While not all authorities recognize subspecies for the rubber boa, most accept *C. b. umbratica* as distinct enough to warrant recognition, and at least one has suggested that it could be considered a separate species.

Rocky Mountain Rubber Boa

Charina bottae utahensis Van Denburgh, 1920

utahensis, Latin = of the state of Utah

Distinguishing Characteristics   This snake usually has 44 or fewer scale rows at midbody and the parietal scale is usually not divided. There are more than 191 ventrals. The supraoculars come to a sharp point between the frontals and parietal scales. The belly is often yellow-orange in color.

Notes   Many authorities consider this subspecies invalid and identical with *C. b. bottae*. Stewart (1977) does not recognize it, but it appears in Stebbins (1985). Collins (1990) lists NO subspecies of the rubber boa.

3 Rosy Boa

Solcuate

Lichanura trivirgata Cope, 1861

Lichanos, Greek = the forefinger; *oura,* Greek = tail; *trivirgata,* Latin = three stripes

Habitat This snake inhabits boulder-strewn, rocky shrublands and deserts. It prefers foothills with numerous rock outcrops or talus slopes and appears to use fissures in rocks as both a resting place and as protection from predators. It is attracted to water that is often found in stream canyons and desert oases, but is not restricted to it.

Figure 2. Rosy boa

This snake occurs up to 3,800 feet in elevation. Unlike the burrowing rubber boa, the rosy is active above ground. It is a good climber.

Prey Like the rubber boa, this snake is not a dietary specialist. It has been observed to eat lizards, small mammals, small birds, and small snakes, even venomous species (Shaw and Campbell, 1974, mention a young sidewinder being consumed by a rosy boa at the San Diego Zoo). Prey is killed by constriction.

Behavior Nocturnal or crepuscular in habits, this snake can be found by night driving along paved roads in rocky canyons or hillsides or by walking with a lantern in such areas at dusk. On cool spring days it can be found abroad in daylight, and it is active on overcast days as well. When irritated, it may coil into a ball as the rubber boa does, but will not use the tail to feign head-like motions. If caught, it will discharge a foul-smelling liquid from glands near the cloacal opening. It seldom attempts to bite.

Reproduction Rosy boas are live-bearing, with 3–12 young born in October or November after 4–5 months gestation. Newborn snakes are 10–14 inches long.

Similar Species Unstriped individuals could perhaps be confused with the rubber boa (2), but their ranges do not overlap, and the lack of large scales on the top of the head in the rosy boa easily distinguishes it.

Subspecies Two subspecies have historically been recognized in California.

Rosy Boa

Lichanura trivirgata

At A Glance

• *Nonvenomous*

• *Size:* 24 to 44 inches (60 to 100 cm)

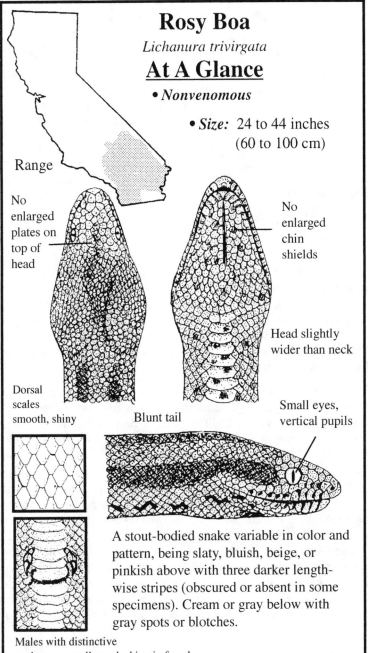

Range

No enlarged plates on top of head

No enlarged chin shields

Head slightly wider than neck

Dorsal scales smooth, shiny

Blunt tail

Small eyes, vertical pupils

A stout-bodied snake variable in color and pattern, being slaty, bluish, beige, or pinkish above with three darker lengthwise stripes (obscured or absent in some specimens). Cream or gray below with gray spots or blotches.

Males with distinctive anal spurs; smaller or lacking in females

Desert Rosy Boa

Lichanura trivirgata gracia Klauber, 1931

gracia, from Gracilis, Latin = gentle

Distinguishing Characteristics   This subspecies has
very distinct stripes that are even-edged, (i.e., straight borders). These stripes are reddish-orange, rose, reddish-brown,
or tan, and contrast with the light gray or beige ground color. There
is seldom spotting of the stripe color on the scales between the
stripes. There is usually some brown flecking on the underside.

Coastal Rosy Boa

Lichanura trivirgata roseofusca Cope, 1868

roseus, Latin = ruddy; *fuscus,* Latin = dusky

Distinguishing Characteristics   Stripes have irregular
borders and are reddish-brown, pink, or dull-brown on a
bluish-gray ground color. The stripe color may also occur as
scattered spots on the scales between the stripes, or occasionally, all
over the dorsal surface. In some specimens, particularly from southwestern San Diego County, the stripes may be obliterated or
obscured by this suffusion of darker color.

Notes   David Spiteri has worked on this genus since the early 1980s
and has come to the conclusion that there is only one subspecies in
California. He calls it the **California Rosy Boa,** *Lichanura trivirgata
myriolepis (myrios,* Greek = numberless, infinite; *lepis,* Greek =
scale) Cope, 1868. He believes that the unicolored specimens found
in southern San Diego County are intergrades between *L. t. myriolepis* and the subspecies found in northwestern Baja California.
This latter snake, he argues, is the snake Cope originally described as
L. t. roseofusca. He considers the subspecies *gracia* to be invalid, as
do several other workers (Yingling, 1982).

   Spiteri's reworking of the rosy boas has gained acceptance among
some herpetologists and many herpetoculturists, but is not accepted
by many others. More time and probably much more work is needed
before the herpetological community finds an acceptable taxonomy.
For more information on Spiteri's work, see *The Vivarium* 5(3): 18-
21, 27, 34.

Family Colubridae: Colubrids

Some authors refer to colubrids as "typical" or "harmless" snakes, but, while this is true within the United States and Canada, outside these regions there are some that are far from harmless! With more than 1,562 species in 292 genera, Colubridae includes most of the snakes found throughout all of the continents except Australia, where elapids (relatives of coral snakes and cobras) outnumber other snakes. Colubridae does not represent a natural grouping, and some authorities recognize at least six separate families within it. Much work remains to be done on the exact relationships among the many species.

Because it contains species in many habitats worldwide, colubrid family members vary greatly in structure and appearance. Therefore it is difficult to characterize the family as a whole. Head scales are usually large and symmetrical. The teeth may be solid or grooved toward the back of the jaw in the so-called "rear-fanged" species. There are no hollow fangs. Some members are venomous, but none in California is dangerous to humans. About 76 percent of California's snakes belong to the Colubridae.

4

Ringneck Snake
(Ring-necked Snake)
Culebra de Collar

Diadophis punctatus (Linnaeus, 1766)

Dia-, Greek = over, across; *ophis*, Greek = snake; *punctatus*, Latin = spotted

Habitat This snake prefers moist habitats and can be found in woodlands, forests, grasslands, chaparral, yards, and gardens. Occasionally it inhabits desert canyons, as long as water is present. It is secretive in its habits and is usually found under surface objects such as rocks, logs (or within rotting logs), the bark of standing or prone dead trees—or under dried "cow pies" (Fowlie, 1965).

Prey Ringneck snakes eat slender salamanders (*Batrachoseps* species), small frogs, tadpoles, lizards, small snakes, slugs, and earthworms. Prey varies among the different subspecies. Some are rather specialized eaters of only one kind of prey (such as slender salamanders), while others are generalists and will eat many kinds of creatures. The rear upper jaw teeth in ringneck snakes are enlarged but not grooved, and their saliva may be venomous to their tiny prey. They pose absolutely no danger to humans and seldom attempt to bite. In most cases they are too small to bite anyway.

Behavior When alarmed, the ringneck snake may coil its tail and flip it over, revealing the bright red underside. Because of its small, smooth scales that desiccate easily, and its preferences in prey, it is more active in cooler and wetter conditions than other snakes.

Reproduction One or possibly two clutches of eggs (one to ten in number), measuring about 7.5 by 32 mm, are laid in June or July. These hatch in 46–60 days. Young are 3.5–5.3 inches (9–13.5 cm) at hatching and grow rapidly, reaching sexual maturity in two or three years.

Similar Species The sharptail snake (5), as its name implies, has a sharp spine at the tip of its tail and alternating light and dark crossbands on its belly. The black-headed snakes (28, 29) usually have a white or beige neck ring and lack black spots on the belly. The reddish color on their belly is bordered on each side by pale gray. Black-headed snakes have no loreal scale.

Notes Ringneck snakes are found in a number of subspecies throughout much of the United States, and there are great variations

Ringneck Snake
Diadophis punctatus
At A Glance

- ***Nonvenomous***

- ***Size:*** 8 to 30 inches, (20 to 75 cm)

Range

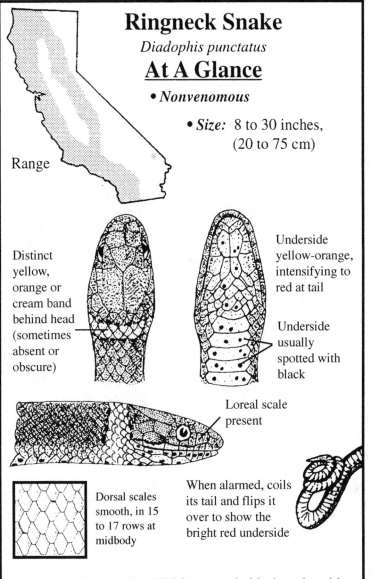

Distinct yellow, orange or cream band behind head (sometimes absent or obscure)

Underside yellow-orange, intensifying to red at tail

Underside usually spotted with black

Loreal scale present

Dorsal scales smooth, in 15 to 17 rows at midbody

When alarmed, coils its tail and flips it over to show the bright red underside

COLUBRIDS

Typically a slender olive, bluish, or nearly black snake with a dark head and a conspicuous neck band. On rare occasions, a black individual is found that lacks both the neck band and orange ventral color, and has dark crossbars on the belly.

in size, color, and eating habits among them. Over the years they have been described as more than one species, and although now they are all considered the same species, more work needs to be done to determine this.

Subspecies Six subspecies are currently recognized in California.

Pacific Ringneck Snake

Diadophis punctatus amabilis Baird & Girard, 1853

amabilis, Latin = lovely

Distinguishing Characteristics In this subspecies the dorsal scale rows are usually 15 and 15 or 15 and 13, counted on neck and at midbody. The orange neck band is 1–1½ scale lengths wide. The red ventral color extends onto ½–1½ rows of the lowermost dorsal scales. There are numerous black spots on the belly.

San Bernardino Ringneck Snake

Diadophis punctatus modestus Bocourt, 1866

modestus, Latin = calm, unassuming, modest

Distinguishing Characteristics The dorsal scale rows are usually 17 and 15, counted at the neck and at midbody. The red ventral color is confined to the first row of dorsal scales. There are conspicuous black dots on the belly.

Northwestern Ringneck Snake

Diadophis punctatus occidentalis Blanchard, 1923

occidentalis, Latin = western

Distinguishing Characteristics The ventral color extends from ½–2 or more rows of the dorsal scales, and this area often has black flecking. The neck band is 1½–3 scales wide. A few small black dots may occur on the belly.

Coralbelly Ringneck Snake

Diadophis punctatus pulchellus Baird & Girard, 1853

pulchellus, Latin = beautiful

Distinguishing Characteristics   This subspecies is similar to the Northwestern Ringneck Snake but without black flecking on the first two rows of dorsal scales. The belly lacks black spotting, or it may be lightly spotted.

San Diego Ringneck Snake

Diadophis punctatus similis Blanchard, 1923

similis, Latin = similar, like (probably so-named because it is similar to other subspecies)

Distinguishing Characteristics   Scale rows usually 15 and 15, or 15 and 13 (the first count is at the neck of the snake and the second is at midbody). The ventral color extends ½–⅔ onto each scale of the first dorsal row.

Monterey Ringneck Snake

Diadophis punctatus vandenburghi Blanchard, 1923

vandenburghi, honoring John Van Denburgh (1872–1924) of the California Academy of Sciences

Distinguishing Characteristics   The dorsal scale rows are usually 17 and 15. A few small black spots occur on the belly.

Notes   There appear to be "coastal" and "inland" forms in this range that differ dramatically in ventral scale counts. No intergrades between the two forms have been found, and this population may actually involve two different species (Sweet, 1997).

COLUBRIDS

5 Sharptail Snake
(Sharp-tailed Snake)

Culebra de Cola Aguda

Contia tenuis (Baird & Girard, 1852)

kontos, Greek = short, a spear or arrow; *tenuis,* Latin = thin, narrow, slender

Habitat   This unique little snake is found in woodland, forest, broken chaparral, and grassland environments, along with pastures or open meadows, usually near streams. It is also found in yards and gardens, particularly in leaf litter, and is sometimes found there by foraging Scrub Jays (McKeown, 1997).

Prey   The sharptail snake apparently feeds mainly on slugs, for which its long teeth are admirably suited. It will readily eat European garden slugs of the genus *Arion* and, in fact, seems to prefer them over native slugs (Rossi and Rossi, 1995). Shaw and Campbell (1974) state that the snake's range may actually be expanding due to the introduction of these slugs by humans (the slug's range expands as new gardens and flower beds are established in human habitations). More field study is needed to ascertain if this is so.

Behavior   Although occasionally found in groups, this secretive snake is seldom seen. It is most active when the ground is damp, but stays out of sight under logs, bark, rocks, or other surface objects. It retreats underground when the weather becomes dry. It is more tolerant of cold temperatures and damp situations than most California snakes.

Reproduction   Since little is known of the reproductive history of this species, it is surmised that the eggs, 2–9 in a clutch probably measuring 6 or 7 mm by 40–46 mm, are laid in June and July, and they probably hatch about two months later.

Similar Species   Melanistic (condition in which dark pigment is accentuated, sometimes obscuring other color) ringneck snakes (4) may resemble the sharptail snake in coloration, even to the barred underside, but the ringneck snake does not have the sharp spine at the tip of the tail that gives the sharptail its common name. The loreal scale is present in the ringneck snake and absent in the sharptail.

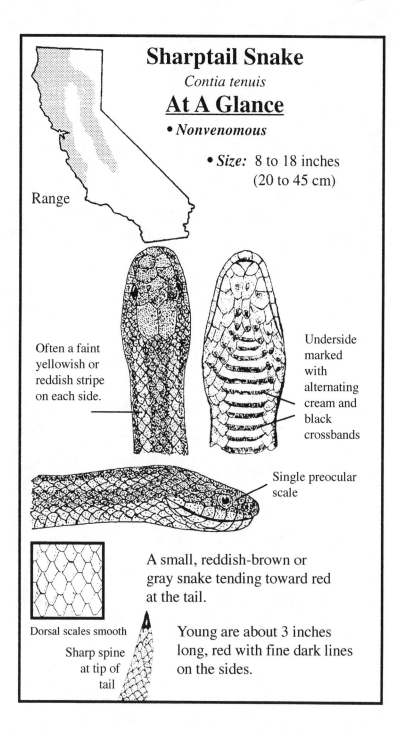

Sharptail Snake

Contia tenuis

At A Glance

• *Nonvenomous*

• *Size:* 8 to 18 inches (20 to 45 cm)

Range

Often a faint yellowish or reddish stripe on each side.

Underside marked with alternating cream and black crossbands

Single preocular scale

A small, reddish-brown or gray snake tending toward red at the tail.

Dorsal scales smooth

Sharp spine at tip of tail

Young are about 3 inches long, red with fine dark lines on the sides.

Notes   The tail spine is harmless to people, although a person unfamiliar with it might be startled into thinking he was bitten or "stung" when probed by it. This spine probably aids the snake in burrowing, as in the blind snakes (*Leptotyphlops*). It has also been suggested that this spine helps to anchor the snake while it struggles to consume a slug.

Contia was once a catchall genus for a number of odd little snakes. One by one the other snakes have been assigned to other genera, including *Chionactis, Conopis, Opheodrys, Pseudoficimia, Seminatrix, Sonora, Toluca,* and the western Asian genus *Eirenis. Contia* is now a monotypic genus, with *C. tenuis* being the sole species.

Subspecies   There are no recognized subspecies of the sharp-tail snake.

6 Spotted Leafnose Snake
(Spotted Leaf-nosed Snake)
Culebra Nariz de Hoja Pinta

Phyllorhynchus decurtatus (Cope, 1868)

Phlylon, Greek = leaf; *rhynchos*, Greek = nose, or snout; *decurto*, Latin = to cut short

In his original description, Cope commented that both "the head is shortened . . ." and that ". . . the tail is relatively shorter . . ."

Habitat   This unusual little snake is found in sandy or gravelly desert areas closely associated with the creosote bush (*Larea divaricata*), although a definite connection between snake and plant cannot be made since each also occurs in areas where the other does not. The modified rostral is apparently used in digging, as when this snake is unearthing lizard eggs, a favorite food.

Prey   The spotted leafnose snake eats small lizards, including banded geckos (*Coleonyx variegatus*) and their eggs. Often the snake may only get the tail of a gecko, which is easily dropped by the lizard when attacked and later regenerated.

Behavior   This snake is nocturnal, and humans rarely encounter it unless they are driving on paved roads in the desert at night. Their major period of activity seems to be April, May, and June between 7:30 P. M. and 10:00 P. M. (Shaw and Campbell, 1974). Little is known of its life history, and it is almost impossible to keep in captivity, so captive observations are also rare. When attacked, the leafnose snake assumes a coiled position, head drawn back appearing ready to strike. It may hiss and strike with its mouth open and its neck expanded vertically, but this is all a bluff—the snake is entirely harmless to humans.

Reproduction   Oviparous, with a clutch of 2–4 eggs presumably laid in June or July. They measure 8–10 mm by 35–37 mm and hatch about two months later. Young are 6–7 inches (15–17 cm) long at hatching.

Similar Species   The Western patchnose snake (11) is the only other California snake with an enlarged rostral scale. The rostral only partly separates the internasals. The patchnose snake has a distinctive broad middorsal stripe.

COLUBRIDS

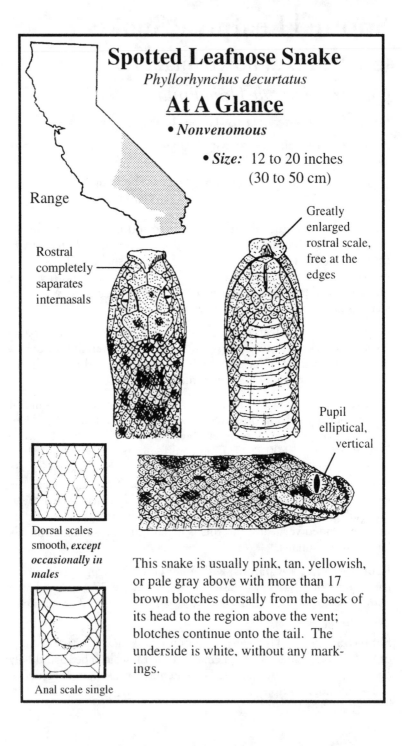

Spotted Leafnose Snake
Phyllorhynchus decurtatus

At A Glance

• *Nonvenomous*

• *Size:* 12 to 20 inches (30 to 50 cm)

Range

Rostral completely saparates internasals

Greatly enlarged rostral scale, free at the edges

Pupil elliptical, vertical

Dorsal scales smooth, *except occasionally in males*

Anal scale single

This snake is usually pink, tan, yellowish, or pale gray above with more than 17 brown blotches dorsally from the back of its head to the region above the vent; blotches continue onto the tail. The underside is white, without any markings.

Notes This snake was first described in 1868, and in the 54 years that followed, only ten specimens were found, leading authorities to believe it was very rare. Then, one night in 1922, Laurence M. Klauber drove slowly along a black-topped desert road. The light color of a spotted leafnose snake stood out in strong contrast to the dark road, making it easy to see. In one night, Klauber doubled the known number of specimens, thus proving that this snake is not at all rare. Since then, "night-driving" has become a routine way to find many nocturnal desert snakes, who are attracted to the pavement's surface by the heat it retains from the daytime.

Subspecies Only one subspecies is found in California.

Western Leaf-nosed Snake

Phyllorhynchus decurtatus perkinsi Klauber, 1935

perkinsi honors Charles B. Perkins, friend and colleague of Klauber's and a former curator of reptiles at the San Diego Zoo

Distinguishing Characteristics This snake is recognized by 24 to 48 dark blotches down the center of the back (excluding its tail). These blotches are narrower than their interspaces.

7 Racer

Corredora

Coluber constrictor Linnaeus, 1758

Coluber, Latin = serpent or snake; *constrictor,* Latin = something that constricts (wholly inappropriate for this species)

Habitat   This snake favors open habitats such as grasslands, pastures and meadows, sagebrush flats, and open chaparral. It is found in semi-arid and moist areas, but not in extremely dry areas. It is rarely found at elevations above 7,000 feet. Quite often it will be found near rocky outcrops or logs that lizards, a main prey item, bask upon. In southern California where such habitats have become buried beneath human developments, south of Ventura County in particular, the species has largely been extirpated.

Prey   In addition to lizards, the racer also eats small mammals, other snakes, frogs, and insects.

Behavior   Moving about in grass or brush, the racer is an active predator that relies heavily on sight in locating prey. Often it will stop and, with head raised high, watch for movement that betrays a lizard's whereabouts. Then, with a final dash of speed, the racer will seize the prey in its mouth, press it down with its body, and commence swallowing (despite the implication of its specific name, it does not constrict prey). The racer is often seen basking and is active at temperatures higher than many other snakes prefer, probably because of its active and speedy lifestyle. Speed is also its first line of defense, dashing away from danger, often after thrashing around violently to attract a predator's attention to a certain piece of ground. It has been said to sometimes circle back around to watch how its ruse has confused its enemy (Shaw and Campbell, 1974). If captured, the racer will thrash violently, striking and biting vigorously.

Reproduction   The racer is oviparous and lays 3–7 eggs between June and August. Eggs are 16–28 mm by 26–40 mm and hatch in 43–65 (average 50) days. Young racers are spotted and brown, which probably conceals them in the dried leaf litter that coats the ground in late summer or early fall when they hatch.

Similar species   Juvenile racers resemble young gopher snakes (14), but have smooth scales and a wedged lower preocular (see page 57). They also resemble the night snake (31), which has vertical pupils.

Subspecies   One subspecies is recognized in California.

Racer

Coluber constrictor

At A Glance

- *Nonvenomous*
  - *Size:* 20 to 73 inches (50 to 182 cm)
    - *A slim snake with large eyes*

Range

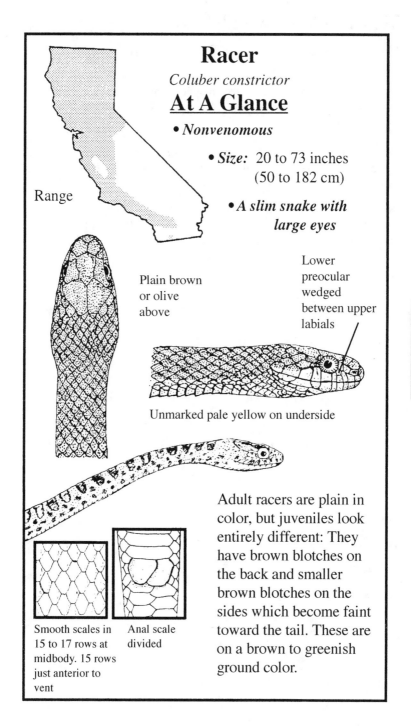

Plain brown or olive above

Lower preocular wedged between upper labials

Unmarked pale yellow on underside

Smooth scales in 15 to 17 rows at midbody. 15 rows just anterior to vent

Anal scale divided

Adult racers are plain in color, but juveniles look entirely different: They have brown blotches on the back and smaller brown blotches on the sides which become faint toward the tail. These are on a brown to greenish ground color.

COLUBRIDS

57

Western Yellowbelly Racer

Coluber constrictor mormon Baird & Girard, 1852

mormon refers to the religious sect inhabiting the area from which the holotype (originally described specimen of the subspecies) came

Distinguishing Characterisitics   This subspecies usually has 8 upper labials and 85 or more caudals. The young have 70–80 dorsal blotches.

Notes   When first discovered, the juvenile Western yellowbelly racer was described as a separate species from the adult—and by the same scientists!

8 Coachwhip

Chirrionera

Masticophis flagellum (Shaw, 1802)

Mastix, Greek = whip; *ophis,* Greek = snake; *flagellum,* Latin = whip

Habitat   The coachwhip is found in a variety of habitats, from creosote bush and mesquite flats to grasslands, oak woodland environments, and farm fields. It prefers open spaces and generally avoids dense vegetation.

Prey   The coachwhip is an active predator that hunts small mammals, birds and their eggs, lizards, snakes and, when young, insects. It has also been known to eat carrion.

Behavior   This is a fast-moving and aggressive snake, more tolerant of warm and dry conditions than other species, so it is often seen abroad by day, even in the desert. If confronted, it will defend itself vigorously, hissing and striking repeatedly. If captured it will nearly always bite, and large individuals are capable of lacerating skin. Like its other relatives, it will course through its habitat with head held high, always alert for any movement that might signify prey or danger.

Reproduction   An egglayer, the coachwhip mates in April or May and lays a clutch of 4–20 eggs, 15–25 mm by 25–57 mm in size, in June or July. Incubation has taken from 45–79 days. Hatchlings are 12–16 inches (30–41 cm) long. Young coachwhips have a blotched or crossbanded pattern of dark brown on a lighter brown ground color.

Notes   Both the scientific and common names refer to this snake's long, thin appearance and the resemblance of the large scales on the tail to a braided whip. In 1714, Captain Thomas Walduck stated, "there be likewise . . . Snakes made like a coachwhip as long and as small, that will twist their head around a horse's leg, and with their tayl lash a horse with great violence untill ye blood comes . . . " Needless to say, this story is totally fictitious.

Subspecies   Three subspecies are recognized in California.

COLUBRIDS

Coachwhip
Masticophis flagellum
At A Glance

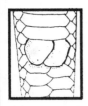

Range

- *Nonvenomous*
  - *Size:* 36 to 102 inches (90 to 255 cm)
  - *Scales on the tail resemble a braided whip*

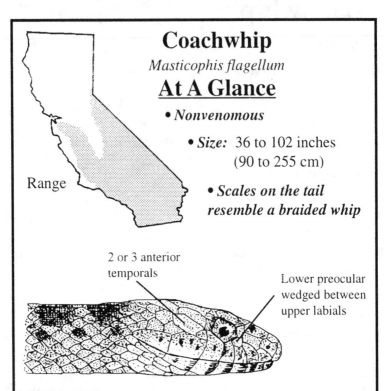

2 or 3 anterior temporals

Lower preocular wedged between upper labials

Smooth scales in 17 rows at midbody, 13 or fewer just anterior to vent

No well-defined lengthwise stripes

The coachwhip's color is highly variable: tan, gray, grayish green, pink, or reddish above, slightly paler below with black crossbars on the neck. Occasional individuals are all black, and specimens from the desert are sometimes yellowish.

Anal scale divided

Baja California Coachwhip

Masticophis flagellum fuliginosus (Cope, 1895)

fuliginis, Latin = soot; *-osus,* Latin = full of, augmented

Distinguishing Characteristics   This subspecies
occurs in both a light phase and a dark phase. The dark
phase enters California in the vicinity of San Diego and is dark
grayish-brown above with light lines on the sides, especially toward the
front. There is a variable amount of cream coloration on the venter.
The light phase is more prevalent in the Cape region of Baja California.
The areas of intergradation between this subspecies and *M. f. piceus*
need further study (Wilson, 1973).

Red Coachwhip (Red Racer)

Masticophis flagellum piceus (Cope, 1892)

piceus, Latin = pitch-black or pitch-brown

Distinguishing Characteristics   This subspecies is
usually reddish or pinkish above, often grading to tan
towards the tail. There are wide black, dark brown, or pink
crossbands on the neck, sometimes more or less united and sometimes faint or absent. Highly variable in color, this snake may be
lighter or darker in various parts of its range. A dark phase (called the
Western black coachwhip) is black above, pale or more or less blackened below, becoming salmon pink to red towards the tail. This
phase is prominent in south-central Arizona.

San Joaquin Coachwhip

Masticophis flagellum ruddocki Brattstrom
and Warren, 1953

ruddocki, named for Dr. John C. Ruddock, medical
director for the Richfield Oil Corporation (which provided
a research grant for the study in which this snake was named)

Status   This subspecies is **PROTECTED** by state law.

Distinguishing Characteristics   This subspecies is light-yellow to
olive-yellow, olive-brown, or occasionally reddish above with neck
bands few or absent. May be light tan below. Its haunts in the San
Joaquin Valley have largely been displaced by agriculture, and oil
exploration and development. Like the Baja California coachwhip,
Wilson (1973) suggests that the areas of intergradation between this
subspecies and *M. f. piceus* are in need of further study.

9 Striped Racer
Culebra Rayada Corredora
Masticophis lateralis (Hallowell, 1853)

Mastix, Greek = whip; *ophis,* Greek = snake; *lateralis,* Latin = of the side (apparently referring to the conspicuous lateral stripes)

Habitat   Mainly found in the chaparral, this snake likes scrublands broken by rocky outcrops, canyons and gullies, and scattered grassy fields. It is chiefly found in the foothills, but ranges into mixed conifer or oak forests in the mountains. It frequents the ecotone (region where vegetative zones meet) between chaparral and riparian (streamside woodland) environments. It is usually found in areas ranging from sea level to about 6,000 feet.

Prey   Not a dietary specialist by any means, the striped racer eats lizards, snakes (including rattlesnakes), small mammals, birds, frogs, and insects. Lizards, particularly spiny lizards, side-blotched lizards, and whiptails (*Sceloporus, Uta,* and *Cnemidophorus* species, respectively) are especially important in the diet.

Behavior   This is an active, diurnal species that may be seen foraging with its head held high, on the lookout for lizards on rocks or tree trunks. It is a good climber and may seek shelter among rocks or in burrows. It is a master at eluding capture, utilizing speed, agility, and climbing skills to escape. If captured, it will thrash violently and bite.

Reproduction   Oviparous, the striped racer lays a clutch of 6–11 eggs between May and July. These measure about 12 by 36 mm. Incubation takes 60–90 days. Young are patterned like the adults.

Similar Species   The striped whipsnake (10) has 15 scale rows at midbody, and each light lateral stripe is bisected by a black line.

Notes   The sharply contrasting stripes on the sides aid them in eluding their enemies because the stripes affect the would-be predator's vision in such a way that the attacker continues to see the snake for a second or two after it has moved away!

Subspecies   Two subspecies are recognized in California.

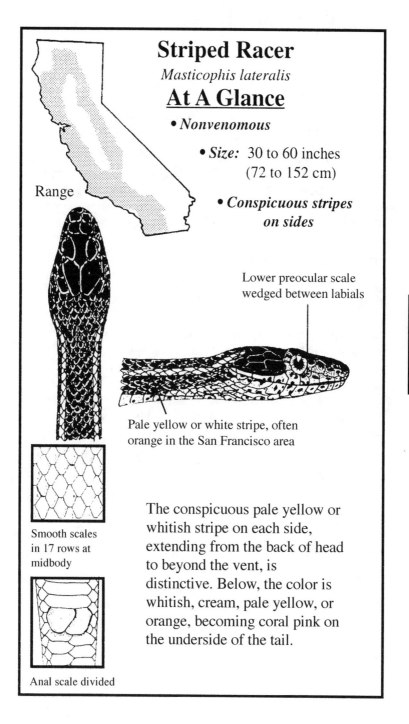

Striped Racer
Masticophis lateralis
At A Glance

- *Nonvenomous*

- *Size:* 30 to 60 inches
(72 to 152 cm)

- *Conspicuous stripes
on sides*

Range

Lower preocular scale
wedged between labials

Pale yellow or white stripe, often
orange in the San Francisco area

Smooth scales
in 17 rows at
midbody

Anal scale divided

The conspicuous pale yellow or whitish stripe on each side, extending from the back of head to beyond the vent, is distinctive. Below, the color is whitish, cream, pale yellow, or orange, becoming coral pink on the underside of the tail.

Alameda Striped Racer

Masticophis lateralis euryxanthus Riemer, 1954

eury-, Greek = wide or broad; *xanthus*, Greek = yellow

Status   The Alameda striped racer is listed as **THREATENED** by the state and is protected by law.

Distinguishing Characteristics   A snake with a sooty black dorsum, broad orange or yellow-orange dorsolateral stripes, and virtually no spotting on the underside of the head and neck. The stripes are 1½–2 scales wide. A heavy suffusion of orange-rufous is present on the anterior pale areas of the underside.

California Striped Racer

Masticophis lateralis lateralis (Hallowell, 1853)

Distinguishing Characteristics   The lateral stripes are cream or yellow, ¼–1 scale in width (or two half-scale rows wide) on an olive-brown, blackish, or dark-brown dorsum. There is heavy spotting on the underside of the head and neck. Often found in the vicinity of ponds, lakes or streams, this snake is a strong swimmer and will not hesitate to take to water if pressed.

Striped Whipsnake

Culebra Látigo Rayada

Masticophis taeniatus (Hallowell, 1852)

Mastix, Greek = whip; *ophis*, Greek = snake; *taeniatus*, Greek = band or ribbon-like striped pattern; thin stripe

Habitat   Like the striped racer (9) to which it is closely related, this snake inhabits sagebrush flats, canyons, and shrubland, grassland, and piñon-juniper and oak woodlands. It likes rocky outcrops and is often attracted to both permanent and intermittent streams. It has been found as high as 9,400 feet in mountains.

Prey   Like other whipsnakes, this species eats lizards, other snakes, small mammals, young birds, and insects. This snake breaks into a sudden burst of speed to capture its prey, which it pins down, if necessary, and then swallows.

Behavior   The striped whipsnake is a fast moving, diurnal snake that seeks shelter in rocky outcrops, burrows, or trees and shrubs (it is a good climber). In behavior and habits it is much like the striped racer (9).

Reproduction   Oviparous, the striped whipsnake lays 3 to 12 eggs in June or July. Eggs measure about 15 mm by 40–45 mm. These hatch in about 2 months. The young are fairly long, 13.75–17 inches (35–43 cm), and resemble the adults.

Similar Species   The striped racer (9) has scales in 17 rows at mid-body, and the light lateral stripes are not bisected by black lines. The ranges of the two species do not overlap.

Subspecies   One subspecies is found in California.

Desert Striped Whipsnake

Masticophis taeniatus taeniatus (Hallowell, 1852)

Distinguishing Characteristics   The head plates of this snake are edged with white, and the underside of the head is white mottled with dark, changing toward the tail to buffs and yellows to coral pink. The mid-dorsal dark area (between the lateral stripes) is 5 and 2-half scales wide. This is a wide-ranging subspecies that occurs from eastern California to western Texas, southeast Washington to northern Mexico.

COLUBRIDS

65

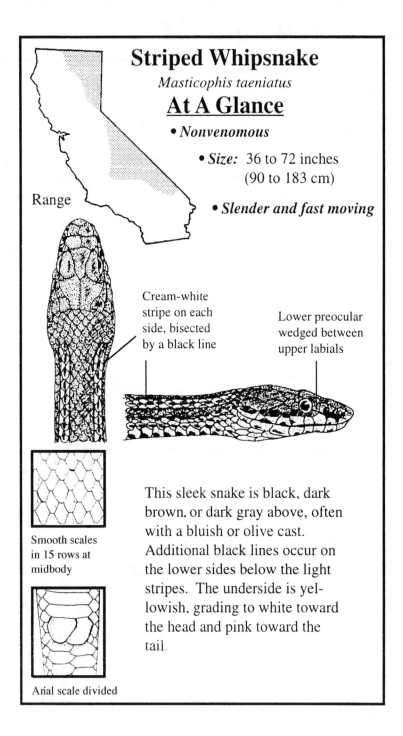

Striped Whipsnake
Masticophis taeniatus
At A Glance

- *Nonvenomous*
  - *Size:* 36 to 72 inches (90 to 183 cm)
    - *Slender and fast moving*

Range

Cream-white stripe on each side, bisected by a black line

Lower preocular wedged between upper labials

Smooth scales in 15 rows at midbody

Anal scale divided

This sleek snake is black, dark brown, or dark gray above, often with a bluish or olive cast. Additional black lines occur on the lower sides below the light stripes. The underside is yellowish, grading to white toward the head and pink toward the tail.

11 Western Patchnose Snake
(Western Patch-nosed Snake)
Cabrastillo
Salvador hexalepis (Cope, 1866)

hex, Greek = six; *lepis,* Greek = scale

Habitat   The Western patchnose snake inhabits brushy desert, sagebrush flats, and grassland, piñon-juniper woodland, and chaparral environments, particularly in sandy or rocky areas. Although the creosote bush and Joshua tree are plants generally associated with this snake's lower elevation habitats, it occasionally goes into higher elevations and has been found at 7,000 feet.

Prey   The patchnose snake eats small mammals, lizards, and reptile eggs, particularly those of lizards. Whiptail lizards, genus *Cnemidophorus,* are particularly important in their diet.

Behavior   A fast-moving, racer-like snake (it is closely related to the racers and whipsnakes) that is chiefly ground-dwelling, but it can also climb agilely into trees or shrubs. It is active diurnally. Like the leafnose snake (6), it uses its enlarged rostral scale as a "shovel" for digging up lizard eggs and whiptail burrows. When approached, this snake tends to freeze and is very hard to see. The coastal subspecies usually does not move at all and can simply be picked up; the desert subspecies seems more wary.

Reproduction   The patchnose snake is an egglayer. A clutch of 4–10 eggs is probably laid between May and August. These measure 9–12 mm by 27–40 mm, and the incubation period appears to be 3–4 months (85 days in the laboratory).

Similar Species   The spotted leafnose snake (6) has a rostral scale that more completely separates the internasals, is blotched dorsally rather than usually striped, and it has an anal scale that is entire.

Notes   Although this species has been studied extensively for its morphology and distinguishing characteristics, little is known about its natural history. There is much to be learned from observations of these snakes in the wild.

Subspecies   Three subspecies occur in California.

COLUBRIDS

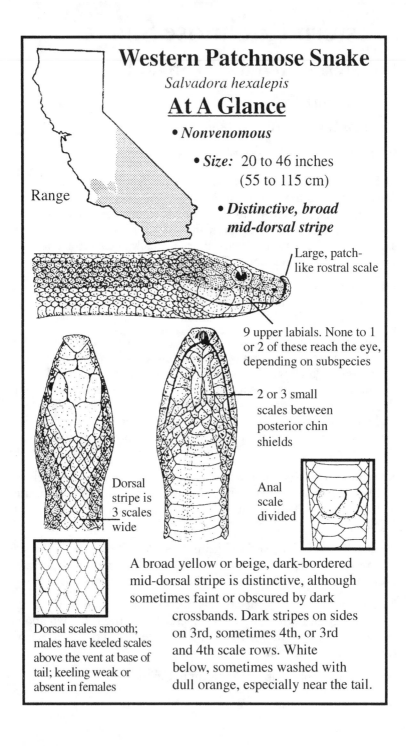

Western Patchnose Snake

Salvadora hexalepis

At A Glance

- *Nonvenomous*
- *Size:* 20 to 46 inches (55 to 115 cm)
- *Distinctive, broad mid-dorsal stripe*

Range

Large, patch-like rostral scale

9 upper labials. None to 1 or 2 of these reach the eye, depending on subspecies

2 or 3 small scales between posterior chin shields

Dorsal stripe is 3 scales wide

Anal scale divided

Dorsal scales smooth; males have keeled scales above the vent at base of tail; keeling weak or absent in females

A broad yellow or beige, dark-bordered mid-dorsal stripe is distinctive, although sometimes faint or obscured by dark crossbands. Dark stripes on sides on 3rd, sometimes 4th, or 3rd and 4th scale rows. White below, sometimes washed with dull orange, especially near the tail.

Desert Patchnose Snake

Salvadora hexalepis hexalepis (Cope, 1866)

Distinguishing Characteristics   One upper labial reaches the eye in this subspecies. The loreal scale is divided. The top of its head is gray, and the median stripe is 3 scale rows wide.

Mojave Patchnose Snake

Salvadora hexalepis mojavensis Bogert, 1945

mojavensis, Latin = of or belonging to the Mojave Desert

Distinguishing Characteristics   This snake's upper labials usually fail to reach the eye. The loreal scale is often divided. The light mid-dorsal stripe is 3 scales wide and extends onto the top of the head. The lower lateral stripes are well defined and occur on the 3rd and 4th dorsal scale rows.

Coast Patchnose Snake

Salvadora hexalepis virgultea (Bogert, 1935)

virgultea, Latin = full of bushes, shrubby

Distinguishing Characteristics   The top of the head is brown in this subspecies. The dorsal stripe is one and two half-scale rows wide (one central scale row with a half-scale row on either side). The sides may be dark, including all but the lowermost one or two scale rows. Usually one upper labial reaches the eye. The loreal is usually divided into two to four scales.

COLUBRIDS

12 Baja California Rat Snake

(Santa Rosalia Rat Snake)

Culebra Ratonera de Baja California (Culebra Amarilla in Southern Baja California)

Bogertophis rosaliae (Mocquard, 1899)

Bogert, for Charles M. Bogert; *ophis,* Greek, = snake; *rosaliae,* from Santa Rosalia, Baja California, the type locality. Bogert was curator of the Department of Herpetology of the American Museum of Natural History from 1943 to 1968, and this genus was named in recognition of his many contributions to the systematics of colubrid snakes.

Habitat   This snake appears to prefer hill slopes and arroyos (washes) generally with rocky outcrops. It seems to frequent areas with springs and streams but has been found in dry areas as well. It is said to be most frequently found in the skirts of dead fronds that envelope palm tree trunks. It is most active after summer rains in the Baja Peninsula.

Prey   Little is known of the natural history of this snake, but its food in captivity suggests that it eats rodents, presumably rats, mice, and other small mammals.

Behavior   Little is known about this snake in the wild. Its collection records suggest that it is nocturnal but not entirely, since it has also been found in daylight.

Reproduction   Nothing is known about the reproductive biology of this snake in the wild. However, it has been extensively bred in captivity in recent years, and much has been learned from captive specimens. Nine to 11 eggs are laid about 9 weeks after copulation, and these hatch in 73–103 days. Young are paler than the adult, with light yellow streaks across the back.

Notes   This is a Baja California (Mexico) species that just barely enters California. A single specimen of this snake was found 1.5 miles east of Mountain Spring, Imperial County, in the early 1980s. It had been found previously at the southern end of Sierra de la Cocopah (Guadalupe Canyon), Baja California Norte, not too far south of the California find. These records, which account for the snake's inclusion in this book, suggest that there could be a (sparse) population of this species in the northern Baja California/extreme southern California area where habitat is suitable.

Subspecies   There are no recognized subspecies of the Baja California rat snake.

Baja California Rat Snake

Bogertophis rosaliae

At A Glance

- *Nonvenomous*

  - *Size:* 34 to 58 inches
    (85 to 145 cm)

    - *Long head,
      slender body*

Range

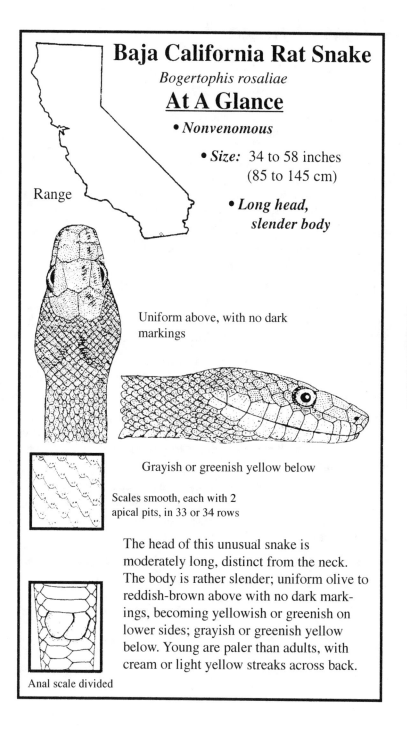

Uniform above, with no dark
markings

Grayish or greenish yellow below

Scales smooth, each with 2
apical pits, in 33 or 34 rows

The head of this unusual snake is
moderately long, distinct from the neck.
The body is rather slender; uniform olive to
reddish-brown above with no dark markings, becoming yellowish or greenish on
lower sides; grayish or greenish yellow
below. Young are paler than adults, with
cream or light yellow streaks across back.

Anal scale divided

13 Glossy Snake

Culebra Brillante

Arizona elegans Kennicott, 1859

Arizona, Latin, from *areo* = dry, and *zona* = a belt of earth; *elegans*, Latin = tasteful, choice, fine, or select

Habitat   This snake can be found in a variety of habitats throughout its range: deserts, both shrubby and barren, sagebrush flats, and chaparral, grassland, and even in woodland environments. It generally prefers open areas, especially those with sandy or loose, loamy soil.

Prey   The glossy snake preys upon lizards especially, but also other snakes and small mammals (especially pocket mice, *Perognathus*), which they kill by constriction.

Behavior   This snake is an excellent burrower and generally remains underground by day, becoming active on the surface at night. Sometimes when farmers plow their fields, they dig up these snakes, which have gone into rodent burrows looking for meals.

Reproduction   The glossy snake is an egglayer, with 3–23 (average 8) white eggs laid in summer. Eggs measure 16–18 mm by 57–63 mm and hatch in 60–72 days. Young are 8–11 inches long.

Similar Species   Gopher snakes (14) have keeled scales. The night snake (31) has a flattened head, distinctly vertical pupils, and a divided anal scale. The lyre snake (30) also has distinctly vertical pupils and a thin neck.

Notes   Some older texts refer to this species as the "Faded Snake." It was once thought to be in the gopher snake genus (*Pituophis*) and was described as having a pattern considerably faded in color compared to other gopher snake species.

Subspecies   Three subspecies are recognized in California.

Glossy Snake

Arizona elegans

At A Glance

• *Nonvenomous*

• *Size:* 26 to 70 inches (66 to 178 cm)
(Seldom exceeds 48 inches in California)

• *Resembles a "faded" gopher snake*

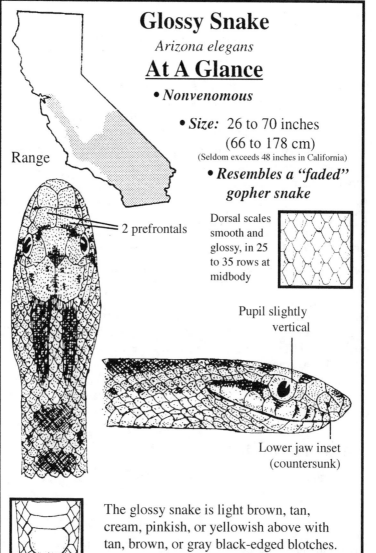

Range

2 prefrontals

Dorsal scales smooth and glossy, in 25 to 35 rows at midbody

Pupil slightly vertical

Lower jaw inset (countersunk)

Anal scale entire

The glossy snake is light brown, tan, cream, pinkish, or yellowish above with tan, brown, or gray black-edged blotches. Its underside is white or pale buff with no markings (although the outer edges of the ventral scales may have some dark markings)

COLUBRIDS

Mojave Glossy Snake

Arizona elegans candida Klauber, 1946

candida, Latin = shining white, bright (refers to the pale
coloration)

Distinguishing Characteristics   There are usually 2
preoculars in this form. This subspecies has 27 or fewer
dorsal scale rows at midbody. There are 203–220 (average 214) ventrals in males, 220–232 (average 223) in females. A series of 53–73
(average 63) narrow blotches occur on the body, about 9 scales wide
at dorsal midline. These blotches are narrower than the spaces
between them.

Desert Glossy Snake

Arizona elegans eburnata Klauber, 1946

eburnata, Latin = of ivory (referring to the light color
pattern)

Distinguishing Characteristics   This snake usually has
one preocular. There are 27 or fewer dorsal scale rows at
midbody. There are 208–238 (average 219) ventrals in males,
220–241 (average 231) in females. This is a pale subspecies with
53–85 (average 68) small, narrow dorsal blotches, narrower than the
spaces between them, and rarely more than 7 scale rows wide at the
dorsal midline.

California Glossy Snake

Arizona elegans occidentalis Blanchard,
1924

occidentalis, Latin = western

Distinguishing Characteristics   This snake usually has
27 rows of dorsal scales. It has 51–75 (average 63) body
blotches. There are dark marks on edges of ventrals, and the lower
labials are often spotted. This is the darkest western subspecies, with
chocolate-colored blotches on a dark tan or brown background.

¹⁴ Gopher Snake

Cincuate

Pituophis catenifer (Blainville, 1835)

Pituitarius, Latin = relating to phlegm or mucus (a reference to its loud hissing–like someone spitting); *ophis,* Greek = snake; *catena,* Latin = chain; *ferre,* Latin = to carry (perhaps in reference to the reticulate dorsal pattern)

Habitat   One of the most common snakes in California, this species is found in a variety of habitats from desert flats to high mountains, from coastal dunes to coniferous forests. It is especially fond of grassland and open brush areas. Soil conditions can be anything from sand or loose loam to hardpan or gravel.

Figure 3. Gopher snake

COLUBRIDS

Prey   Gopher snakes are among the most valuable of snakes in terms of "pest" control, consuming large numbers of rodents (including gophers, rats, mice, voles, and ground squirrels), rabbits, birds and their eggs, and occasionally insects and lizards. The snake kills its prey by constriction.

Behavior   This snake is largely active by day, although when it is hotter in desert regions, it becomes nocturnal. It is a good burrower and climber. When alarmed it will coil and strike, flatten its head, hiss loudly, and vibrate its tail against the ground. This behavior is used to confuse predators, but unfortunately it sometimes causes people to kill it out of fear.

Reproduction   One or two clutches of eggs, 2–24 eggs each, are laid June through August. The eggs measure about 30 by 90 mm and hatch in 52–85 days. Hatchlings are large enough to eat small mice– 10.25–17.7 inches (26–45 cm) in length. Wild snakes are thought to reach sexual maturity in 3–4 years.

Similar Species   The blotched young of the racer (7) resembles a gopher snake, but it has smooth scales and large eyes; the glossy snake (13) also has smooth scales and is usually lighter in color and pattern; the Western rattlesnake (37) has one or more blunt scales (the rattle) at the end of the tail and, at rest, a definitely triangular head.

Gopher Snake
Pituophis catenifer
<u>At A Glance</u>

• *Nonvenomous*

• *Size:* 36 to 110 inches
(90 to 275 cm)
(Seldom exceeds 72 inches in California)

• *Common large,
blotched snake*

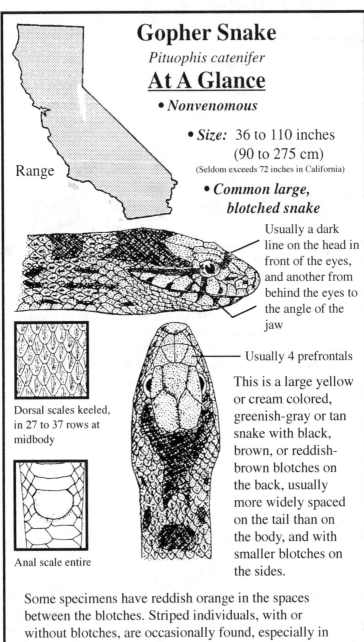

Range

Usually a dark line on the head in front of the eyes, and another from behind the eyes to the angle of the jaw

Dorsal scales keeled, in 27 to 37 rows at midbody

Anal scale entire

Usually 4 prefrontals

This is a large yellow or cream colored, greenish-gray or tan snake with black, brown, or reddish-brown blotches on the back, usually more widely spaced on the tail than on the body, and with smaller blotches on the sides.

Some specimens have reddish orange in the spaces between the blotches. Striped individuals, with or without blotches, are occasionally found, especially in central and south central California.

Notes   Gopher snakes are popular "pet" snakes, usually becoming docile in captivity and always reliable eaters. They are one of three species currently allowed by California law to be bred for commercial purposes by people with proper permits (the other two are the rosy boa and the common kingsnake). There have been several "color morphs" (such as albinos) developed by breeders for the pet trade.

Subspecies   Five subspecies are recognized in California.

Sonoran Gopher Snake

Pituophis catenifer affinis Hallowell, 1852

affinis, Latin = related by marriage (perhaps in
reference to its affinity to *P. c. sayi,* the bullsnake of the
Midwest)

Distinguishing Characteristics   The rostral scale is broad
in this subspecies, raised only slightly (if at all) above the adjacent scales. The ground color of the sides is the same as that of the back, with no gray wash or suffusion of gray spots. The dorsal blotches toward the front of the body are brown, unconnected to other blotches. Blotches darken toward the rear of the snake.

San Diego Gopher Snake

Pituophis catenifer annectens Baird &
Girard, 1853

annectens, Latin = to connect (perhaps in reference to
the confluent neck blotches)

Distinguishing Characteristics   In general, this snake
resembles the Pacific gopher snake, but the dorsal blotches
toward the front are black and more or less joined to one another
and to the secondary lateral blotches.

Pacific Gopher Snake

Pituophis catenifer catenifer (Blainville, 1835)

Distinguishing Characteristics   There is a suffusion
of grayish dots (or a gray "wash") on the sides of the
body and on the underside of the tail. The dorsal blotches toward the front of the body are brown or black, separated
from one another and from the secondary blotches on the sides.

COLUBRIDS

Great Basin Gopher Snake

Pituophis catenifer deserticola Stejneger, 1893

deserere, Latin = to desert or abandon; *cola*, Latin = inhabitant (a reference to this subspecies' occurrence in desert regions)

Distinguishing Characteristics   This subspecies resembles the Sonoran gopher snake, but the dorsal blotches toward the front of the body are usually black (blotches are gray with black edging in young) and connected to one another and to the secondary blotches on the side of the neck, forming a lateral dark band, which leaves the interspaces as isolated pale dorsal blotches.

Santa Cruz Gopher Snake (Channel Island Gopher Snake)

Pituophis catenifer pumilis Klauber, 1946

pumilio, Latin = a dwarf (refers to the small size of the adults)

Distinguishing Characteristics   A dwarf race seldom exceeding three feet in length. This subspecies usually has 29 or fewer dorsal scale rows at midbody (other subspecies usually have more than 29). There are no black-streaked scales toward the front of the body in the light spaces between the dorsal blotches. This subspecies is found only on Santa Cruz, Santa Rosa, and San Miguel islands off the south-central California coast.

This snake is known in most references as the Santa Cruz gopher snake, but in deference to the fact that it occurs on two other islands, and to avoid confusion with Santa Cruz on mainland California, I'd like to see the name Channel Island Gopher Snake come into common usage (the three islands it inhabits are part of Channel Islands National Park).

¹⁵ Common Kingsnake

Culebra Real Común

Lampropeltis getula (Linnaeus, 1766)

Lampros, Greek = shiny; *pelta,* Greek = shield; *getula,* = belonging to the Getulians (a people inhabiting northwestern Africa in ancient times; a misnomer based on the mistaken thought that this snake had been found in Morocco)

Habitat   The common kingsnake is found in a variety of habitats: forests, woodland, grassland, and chaparral environments, marshes, river bottoms, valleys, deserts, and farmlands. It is often found near rocky outcrops and clumps of vegetation, under rocks, logs, boards, or other surface debris. Its common name is fitting, as it is indeed a common snake.

Prey   The common kingsnake is most noted for eating rattlesnakes, which endears it with the public as no other snake can. However, although that is true, they also eat other harmless snakes, lizards, reptile eggs, birds and their eggs, and small mammals, small turtles, and frogs. They are hardly dietary specialists!

Behavior   Chiefly active by day, especially the morning and late afternoon hours, except when the weather is very hot, when it may become active at night. This snake is usually terrestrial but may occasionally climb into shrubs. It is usually gentle but sometimes hisses, strikes, and vibrates its tail. When attacked, it sometimes rolls into a ball with its head in the center and everts the lining of its vent, smearing its tormentor with feces and a foul-smelling musk.

Reproduction   The kingsnake is an egg-layer with a clutch of 2–24 eggs usually produced from May to August. Eggs measure 18–30 mm by 35–69 mm. Incubation varies from 47–81 days (average 71 days in the laboratory). Hatchlings are 8–13 inches (20.2–33 cm) in length. They reach sexual maturity in 3–4 years.

Similar Species   The California mountain kingsnake (16) that inhabits the Sierra Nevada range sometimes has reduced or, rarely, no red in its markings, but the white bands usually do not widen on the lower sides; in the longnose snake (17), some or all of the subcaudals are undivided.

Notes   At one time, a color variation inhabiting southeastern California and southwestern Arizona was called the Yuma kingsnake, *L. g. yumensis,* after the city in the area. The snake is very dark, with

COLUBRIDS

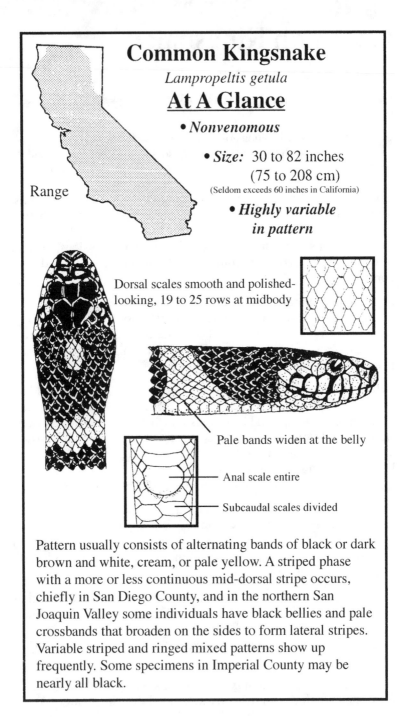

Common Kingsnake
Lampropeltis getula
At A Glance
- *Nonvenomous*

- *Size:* 30 to 82 inches
(75 to 208 cm)
(Seldom exceeds 60 inches in California)

- *Highly variable
in pattern*

Range

Dorsal scales smooth and polished-looking, 19 to 25 rows at midbody

Pale bands widen at the belly

Anal scale entire

Subcaudal scales divided

Pattern usually consists of alternating bands of black or dark brown and white, cream, or pale yellow. A striped phase with a more or less continuous mid-dorsal stripe occurs, chiefly in San Diego County, and in the northern San Joaquin Valley some individuals have black bellies and pale crossbands that broaden on the sides to form lateral stripes. Variable striped and ringed mixed patterns show up frequently. Some specimens in Imperial County may be nearly all black.

very narrow light crossbands. The subspecies is now considered invalid, and Yuma kings are yet another variation of the malleable California kingsnake, although they may constitute intergrades with *L. g. nigrita,* the black kingsnake of Mexico.

Subspecies   One subspecies is currently recognized in California.

California Kingsnake

Lampropeltis getula californiae,
(Blainville, 1835)

californiae, Latin = of California

Distinguishing Characteristics   This snake occurs in two basic patterns, banded and striped, with many intermediate forms. The four photographs in the color section demonstrate some of the variety of patterns in this snake. At one time the striped phase was thought to be a separate subspecies, described as *L. g. californiae,* while the usual banded phase was known as *L. g. boylei,* until both patterns were observed hatching from a single clutch of eggs!

16 California Mountain Kingsnake

Culebra Real de Montaña California

Lampropeltis zonata (Blainville, 1835)

Lampros, Greek = shiny; *pelta,* Greek = shield; *zonata,* Latin = banded

Habitat   The California mountain kingsnake inhabits moist woods, coniferous forests, oak woodland and chaparral, not just in mountains but in canyons down to sea level. It is generally found in south-facing rocky areas near streams, especially where there are rotting logs.

Prey   The California mountain kingsnake is a dietary generalist, eating a variety of prey items from lizards and other snakes to bird eggs and nestlings and small mammals.

Behavior   This snake is chiefly diurnal, but becomes crepuscular to nocturnal during very warm weather. It spends much of the time beneath granite and sandstone slabs. It is a good climber. When captured, it will writhe about in an attempt to escape, smear its captor with the smelly contents of its cloaca, and usually will attempt to bite.

Reproduction   A clutch of 3–9 eggs is laid in June or July. These eggs hatch in August or September after an incubation of 48–87 days. Hatchlings measure 7.9–10.5 inches (20–26.7 cm) in length.

Similar Species   The longnose snake (17) has some or most of its subcaudal scales undivided.

Notes   This snake has sometimes been called the "coral" kingsnake because of its superficial resemblance to the venomous coral snakes. There are no coral snakes in California, however, and using the name mountain kingsnake avoids misunderstandings. The mountain kingsnake is, of course, harmless, and is one of the most beautiful of all serpents, drawing grudging grunts of admiration even from confirmed snake haters.

Subspecies   Five subspecies are currently recognized in California. Additional study still needs to be done to determine the relationships and specific status of these populations, particularly those isolated from others.

A specific term is used in describing the pattern of these snakes—*triad.* A triad is a black ring split by red, or a trio of rings, black-red-

California Mountain Kingsnake

Lampropeltis zonata

At A Glance

- *Nonvenomous*
- *Size:* 21 to 48.25 inches (53 to 120 cm)
- *A "living jewel"*

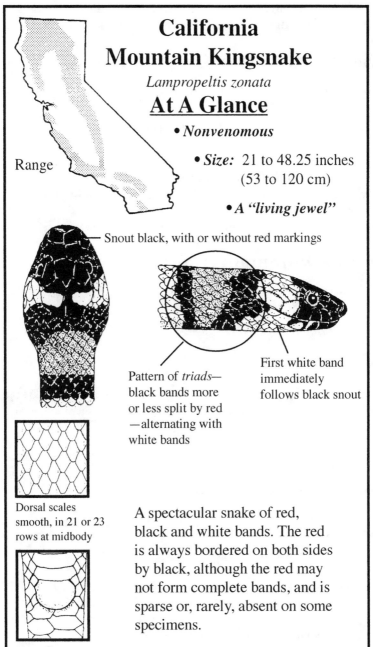

Range

Snout black, with or without red markings

Pattern of *triads*— black bands more or less split by red —alternating with white bands

First white band immediately follows black snout

Dorsal scales smooth, in 21 or 23 rows at midbody

Anal scale entire

A spectacular snake of red, black and white bands. The red is always bordered on both sides by black, although the red may not form complete bands, and is sparse or, rarely, absent on some specimens.

black. It is the number of these triads, each separated by a white ring, that helps determine the subspecies as they are currently described.

Sierra Mountain Kingsnake

Lampropeltis zonata multicincta
(Yarrow, 1882)

multis, Latin = many; *cinctus,* Latin = banded

Distinguishing Characteristics   In this subspecies, the rear edge of the first white band on the head is located behind the corner of the mouth. There are 23–48 (average 35) body triads, usually fewer than 60% of the triads split by red (sometimes the red is completely absent).

Coast Mountain Kingsnake

Lampropeltis zonata multifasciata
(Bocourt, 1886)

multus, Latin = many; *fascis,* Latin = a bundle or band

Distinguishing Characteristics   The rear edge of the first white band on the head may be located behind or in front of the corner of the mouth. There are 26–45 (average 35) body triads, 60% or more completely split by red in this form. The snout usually has some red markings.

San Bernardino Mountain Kingsnake

Lampropeltis zonata parvirubra
Zweifel, 1952

parvus, Latin = little; *ruber,* Latin = red

Distinguishing Characteristics   The rear edge of the first white band on the head of this snake is located on or in front of the last upper labial. It has 35–56 (average 41) body triads, usually fewer than 60% split by red. The snout is dark.

San Diego Mountain Kingsnake

Lampropeltis zonata pulchra Zweifel, 1952

pulchra, Latin = beautiful

Status   The San Diego mountain kingsnake is **PRO-TECTED** by Fish and Game laws and may not be taken or possessed without a special permit. No California mountain kingsnakes may be taken in San Diego or Orange counties, or in Los Angeles County west of Interstate 5.

Distinguishing Characteristics   The first white band on the head of this subspecies is the same as in the San Bernardino mountain kingsnake. It has 26–39 (average 33) body triads, usually 60% or more of them split by red. The snout is dark.

Saint Helena Mountain Kingsnake

Lampropeltis zonata zonata (Blainville, 1835)

Distinguishing Characteristics   The first white band is the same as the San Bernardino and San Diego mountain kingsnakes, but this subspecies has 24–30 (average 27) body triads, usually 60% or more completely split by red. The snout is dark. The black pigment bordering the red on the sides is usually more than one scale wide.

COLUBRIDS

85

¹⁰ Longnose Snake

(Long-nosed Snake)

Culebra de Nariz-larga

Rhinocheilus lecontei Baird & Girard, 1853

Rhino, Greek = nose; *cheilo,* Greek = lip; *lecontei,* honoring the naturalist John L. LeConte

Habitat This snake prefers rocky or brushy habitat and is found in desert, grassland, and scrubland areas where these conditions are present. It seldom ranges higher than 4,000 feet elevation, although it has been found as high as 5,400 feet. Although common, this snake is seldom seen during daylight, because it remains beneath the surface or under objects during that time. Although living in basically arid regions, this snake is attracted to moisture and is drawn to irrigated lands in the deserts.

Prey Lizards and their eggs, small snakes [a particular favorite seems to be the ground snake (26), at least in captive situations (Rossi and Rossi, 1994)], small mammals, and perhaps small birds. Prey is killed by constriction.

Behavior This snake is crepuscular to nocturnal and is likely to be found on paved roadways at night. Surprisingly, for a lower-elevation dweller, it appears to be active at lower temperatures. Klauber reports finding one being blown across a desert road at night in a strong, cold wind when no other snakes were about (Shaw and Campbell, 1974). It is a good burrower, aided by its pointed snout. When alarmed it may vibrate its tail, writhe the hind part of its body, and evert its vent lining, smearing its tormentor with blood and feces. This release of blood seems to occur in females only for reasons not entirely understood (Shaw and Campbell, 1974).

Reproduction The longnose snake is oviparous and lays one, perhaps two clutches of 4–11 eggs, from June to August. Some authorities believe that they lay eggs only every other year. In all probability, the number of clutches and times they are laid depends on prevailing environmental conditions and the physical well-being of the snake itself. Still, here is another area open for study. The eggs measure 7–16 mm by 20–36 mm and hatch in 65–83 days. Hatchlings are 6.7–11 inches (17–28 cm) in length. The red coloration on young, when present, is lighter than that of adults, and there is less speckling, but otherwise they resemble the adult snakes.

Longnose Snake

Rhinocheilus lecontei

At A Glance

- *Nonvenomous*

  - *Size:* 20 to 41 inches (50 to 104 cm)

  - *A slim, speckled snake*

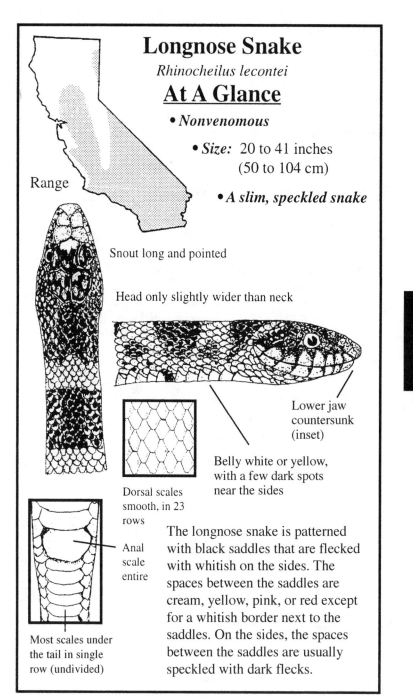

Range

Snout long and pointed

Head only slightly wider than neck

Lower jaw countersunk (inset)

Dorsal scales smooth, in 23 rows

Belly white or yellow, with a few dark spots near the sides

Anal scale entire

Most scales under the tail in single row (undivided)

The longnose snake is patterned with black saddles that are flecked with whitish on the sides. The spaces between the saddles are cream, yellow, pink, or red except for a whitish border next to the saddles. On the sides, the spaces between the saddles are usually speckled with dark flecks.

COLUBRIDS

87

Similar Species The common kingsnake (15) and the California mountain kingsnake (16) both have divided subcaudals.

Notes In some parts of its range, a color phase of this snake occurs that is strongly black and white banded, with no red in the interspaces and little dark flecking on the sides; thus, it greatly resembles a common kingsnake. This phase was once described as a subspecies, *R. l. clarus,* until individuals both with and without red were observed to hatch from a single clutch of eggs.

Subspecies One subspecies occurs in California.

Western Longnose Snake

Rhinocheilus lecontei lecontei Baird & Girard, 1853

Distinguishing Characteristics This snake actually has a shorter snout than its cousin, the Texas longnose snake, and its snout is not upturned. The black saddles in the "clarus" color phase of this subspecies are longer and fewer than in those with the typical reddish coloring in the interspaces.

1. **Western blind snake**
   Leptotyphlops humilis

2. **Rubber boa**
   Charina bottae

Dennis Sheridan

3a. **Rosy boa**
   (Desert rosy boa)
   Lichanura trivirgata

Philip Brown

3b. **Rosy boa**
   (Coastal rosy boa)
   Lichanura trivirgata

4. Ringneck snake
Diadophis punctatus

5. Sharptail snake
Contia tenuis

6. **Spotted leafnose snake**
Phyllorhynchus decurtatus

7. **Racer**
(Western yellowbelly racer)
Coluber constrictorr mormon

8a. **Coachwhip**
    (Red coachwhip)
    Masticophis flagellum piceus

8b. **Coachwhip**
    (Red coachwhip)
    Masticophis flagellum piceus

Paul Collins

8c. Coachwhip
  (San Joaquin coachwhip)
  Masticophis flagellum ruddocki

W. J. Houck

9. Striped racer
  Masticophis lateralis

10. Striped whipsnake
(Desert-striped whipsnake)
Masticophis taeniatus taeniatus

11. Western patchnose snake
Salvadora hexalepis

12. Baja California rat snake
Bogertophis rosaliae

13. Glossy snake
Arizona elegans

14a. Gopher snake
   (Sonoran gopher snake)
   Pituophis catenifer affinis

14b. Gopher snake
   (San Diego gopher snake)
   Pituophis catenifer annectens

14c. Gopher snake
    (Pacific gopher snake)
    Pituophis catenifer catenifer

14d. Gopher snake
    (Great Basin gopher snake)
    Pituophis catenifer deserticola

Paul Collins

14e. Gopher snake
   (Santa Cruz gopher snake)
   Pituophis catenifer pumilis

Dennis Sheridan

15a. Common kingsnake
   (California kingsnake)
   Lampropeltis getula californiae

15b. **Common kingsnake**
    (California kingsnake)
    Lampropeltis getula californiae

15c. **Common kingsnake**
    (California kingsnake)
    Lampropeltis getula californiae

15d. **Common kingsnake**
    (California kingsnake)
    Lampropeltis getula californiae

15e. **Common kingsnake (left)**
    Lampropeltis getula and
    Sidewinder
    Crotalus cerastes (Common kingsnakes are known to eat other snakes,
    including rattlers.)   101

16a. California mountain kingsnake
   (Sierra mountain kingsnake)
   Lampropeltis zonata multicincta

16b. California mountain kingsnake
   (Coast mountain kingsnake)
   Lampropeltis zonata multifasciata

Ian Recchio

16c. California mountain kingsnake
   (San Bernardino mountain kingsnake)
   Lampropeltis zonata parvirubra

Philip Brown

16d. California mountain kingsnake
   (San Diego mountain kingsnake)
   Lampropeltis zonata pulchra

17. **Longnose snake**
   Rhinocheilus lecontei

18a. **Common garter snake**
   (**California red-sided garter snake**)
   Thamnophis sirtalis infernalis

18b. Common garter snake
    (San Francisco garter snake)
    Thamnophis sirtalis tetrataenia

19a. Western terrestrial garter snake
    (Mountain garter snake)
    Thamnophis elegans elegans

105

19b. Western terrestrial garter snake
     (Coast garter snake)
     Thamnophis elegans terrestris

19c. Western terrestrial garter snake
     (Wandering garter snake)
     Thamnophis elegans vagrans

20a. Western aquatic garter snake
   (Santa Cruz garter snake)
   Thamnophis atratus atratus

20b. Western aquatic garter snake
   (Oregon garter snake)
   Thamnophis atratus hydrophilus

21. **Sierra garter snake**
   Thamnophis couchii

22. **Giant garter snake**
   Thamnophis gigas

Ian Recchio

23. Two-striped garter snake
Thamnophis hammondii

Suzanne L. Collins
The Center for North American Amphibians and Reptiles

24. Northwestern garter snake
Thamnophis ordinoides

25. Checkered garter snake
Thamnophis marcianus

26a. Ground snake
Sonora semiannulata

26b. **Ground snake**
Sonora semiannulata

27. **Western shovel-nosed snake**
Chionactis occipitalis

28. **Western black-headed snake**
   Tantilla planiceps

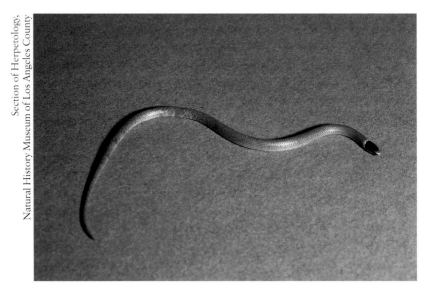

29. **Southwestern black-headed snake**
   Tantilla hobartsmithi

30a. **Lyre snake (Sonoran lyre snake)**
Trimorphodon biscutatus lambda
(specimen is preparing to shed)

30b. **Lyre snake**
   (California lyre snake)
   Trimorphodon biscutatus vandenburghi

31. **Night snake**
Hypsiglena torquata

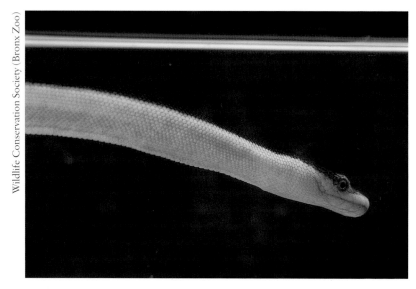

32. **Yellowbelly sea snake**
Pelamis platurus

33. Western diamondback rattlesnake
    Crotalus atrox

34. Red diamond rattlesnake
    Crotalus exsul

35a. Speckled rattlesnake
    (Southwestern speckled rattlesnake)
    Crotalus mitchelli pyrrhus

35b. Speckled rattlesnake
    (Panamint rattlesnake)
    Crotalus mitchelli stephensi

Philip Brown

36. Sidewinder
   Crotalus cerastes

Philip Brown

37a. Western rattlesnake
   (Southern Pacific rattlesnake)
   Crotalus viridis helleri

37b. **Western rattlesnake**
    (Southern Pacific rattlesnake)
    Crotalus viridis helleri

37c. **Western rattlesnake**
    (Great Basin rattlesnake)
    Crotalus viridis lutosus

37d. Western rattlesnake
    (Northern Pacific rattlesnake)
    Crotalus viridis oreganus

37e. Western rattlesnake (Northern Pacific rattlesnake)
    Crotalus viridis oreganus (babies)

37f. **Western rattlesnake**
   (Northern Pacific rattlesnake)
   Crotalus viridis oreganus

38. **Mojave rattlesnake**
   Crotalus scutulatus

¹⁸ Common Garter Snake

Culebra de Agua Nómada Común

Thamnophis sirtalis (Linnaeaus, 1758)

Thamnos, Greek = a bush, shrub; *ophis,* Greek = snake; *sirtalis,* Latin = like a garter

Status *Thamnophis sirtalis* may not be taken in Ventura, Los Angeles, Orange, Riverside, and San Diego counties.

Habitat The common garter snake is so named because it is found throughout much of the United States and southern Canada. In fact, it has the most northward range of any snake in the Western Hemisphere. In California, it is found in many environments—grassland, woodland, chaparral, and riparian areas or marshlands—as long as there is water nearby. This snake seldom moves away from the water, using it as an avenue of escape when threatened, as well as a source for most of its prey.

Prey This species eats fish, toads and frogs, tadpoles, salamanders, earthworms, slugs, leeches, and perhaps small mammals. It has also been reported to eat crayfish and even other snakes—including its own kind (Rossi and Rossi, 1994).

Behavior This snake may have the longest activity season and coldest temperature tolerance of any North American snake. It has been found abroad in temperatures ranging from 48° to 95° F (9° to 35 ° C), although its preferred temperature range appears to be 68° to 95° F (20° to 35° C). When caught, this snake will defend itself vigorously by biting and smearing its captors with feces and the particularly unpleasant smelling contents of its anal glands (a common defense of many snakes, particularly of the *Thamnophis* species).

Reproduction Garter snakes are live-bearing, and this species may produce 3–85 (often 12–18) young any time between May and October. Young snakes measure 5.3–9.1 inches (13.5–23 cm) at birth.

Similar Species The usual presence of red markings between the stripes, 7 (occasionally 8) upper labials, and relatively large eyes distinguish this species from other garter snakes within its range.

Notes As mentioned in the key, identifying garter snakes can be a confusing and frustrating task.

Subspecies Three subspecies are recognized in California. It is worth noting here that Rossman, Ford, and Seigel (1996) do not rec-

COLUBRIDS

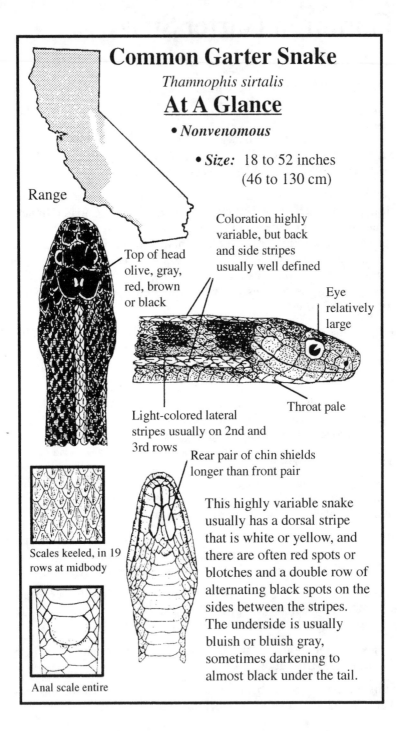

Common Garter Snake

Thamnophis sirtalis

At A Glance

• *Nonvenomous*

• *Size:* 18 to 52 inches (46 to 130 cm)

Range

Top of head olive, gray, red, brown or black

Coloration highly variable, but back and side stripes usually well defined

Eye relatively large

Light-colored lateral stripes usually on 2nd and 3rd rows

Throat pale

Rear pair of chin shields longer than front pair

Scales keeled, in 19 rows at midbody

Anal scale entire

This highly variable snake usually has a dorsal stripe that is white or yellow, and there are often red spots or blotches and a double row of alternating black spots on the sides between the stripes. The underside is usually bluish or bluish gray, sometimes darkening to almost black under the tail.

ognize the subspecies *T. s. tetrataenia;* they refer to it as *T. s. infer-nalis* and consider the California red-sided garter snake as *T. s. concinnus.* This position has been questioned by Barry, Jennings, and Smith (1996), who feel that such changes will result in "major and unwarranted disruption of western garter snake taxonomy" and will further adversely impact conservation efforts for the San Francis-co garter snake. They have petitioned the International Commission on Zoological Nomenclature to conserve the accepted usage and have reminded workers who cite the names for these snakes to main-tain the pre-1995 usage, as required by Article 80 of the International Code of Zoological Nomenclature, until the ruling of the Commis-sion is published. In keeping with that request, I am herein using the nomenclature that has been in acceptance for more than 45 years.

Valley Garter Snake

Thamnophis sirtalis fitchi Fox, 1951

fitchi, honors the herpetologist Henry S. Fitch

Distinguishing Characteristics   The ground color of this snake is slaty, black, or brownish. Its dorsal stripe is broad with regular, well-defined borders. The top of the head is black or dark gray. Black coloration on the belly is usually confined to the edges of the ventrals.

California Red-sided Garter Snake

Thamnophis sirtalis infernalis
(Blainville, 1835)

infernalis, Latin = of Hell, abominable

Distinguishing Characteristics   This snake's ground color is dark gray to black, with indistinct dark spots on the back. Three stripes—one mid-dorsal and one on each side—are bright greenish yel-low, those on the sides often merging into the ventral color. Red or orange bars or spots of varying size and intensity occur between the stripes.

San Francisco Garter Snake

Thamnophis sirtalis tetrataenia
(Cope, 1875)

tetrataenia, Greek = four-striped (refers to the dorsal color areas)

Status   The San Francisco garter snake is listed as **ENDANGERED** by both the state and federal governments under the Endangered Species Act. It has full protection of the law.

Distinguishing Characteristics   This distinctive subspecies has a wide dorsal stripe of greenish yellow edged with black, bordered on each side by a broad red stripe, which is itself followed with a black stripe. The belly is greenish blue, and the top of the head is red or rust colored.

Notes   Before urban sprawl in the mid-1900s, this snake was quite common throughout the Bay area, including the East Bay, San Francisco, and the Peninsula.

19

Western Terrestrial Garter Snake

Culebra de Agua Nómada Occidental Terrestre

Thamnophis elegans (Baird & Girard, 1853)

Thamnos, Greek = a bush, shrub; *ophis,* Greek = snake; *elegans,*
Latin = elegant

Habitat   This garter snake occurs in a variety of habitats–grassland, chaparral, woodland, and open forest areas. As the common name implies, it is often more terrestrial than aquatic; nevertheless, it is usually found in the vicinity of fresh water.

Prey   A rather non-select feeder, the western terrestrial garter snake feeds on slugs, snails, leeches, earthworms, fish, frogs and toads, tadpoles, lizards, small snakes, small mammals, occasionally birds, insects, and carrion.

Behavior   When frightened, this snake may retreat into heavy vegetation or among rocks, or into nearby water. Like other garter snakes, when captured it will smear its captor with fecal matter and a smelly musk.

Reproduction   Like all garter snakes, this species is live-bearing, with 4–12 (record 19) young born from July through September. They measure from 5–10.9 inches (12.7–27.6 cm). Farther north, litter sizes in this species tend to be smaller.

Similar Species   The distinct dorsal stripe will usually distinguish this species in areas where it overlaps with the western aquatic garter snake (20) and the Sierra garter snake (21). East of the Sierra Nevada crest there may be difficulty discerning between the wandering garter snake subspecies of this snake and the Sierra garter snake (21). The latter has a narrow, dull dorsal stripe, ordinarily confined to the anterior region of the body, and is checkered with large, squarish spots. The wandering garter snake usually has a wider stripe that runs the full length of the body, and the spots are rounder and well separated.
  Where the Santa Cruz garter snake subspecies of the Western aquatic garter snake (20) overlaps the range of the Coast subspecies of this snake, the Santa Cruz garter snake usually has an orange rather than yellow dorsal stripe and generally a golden to orange suffusion of color or blotches on the ventrals. In addition, the western aquatic

COLUBRIDS

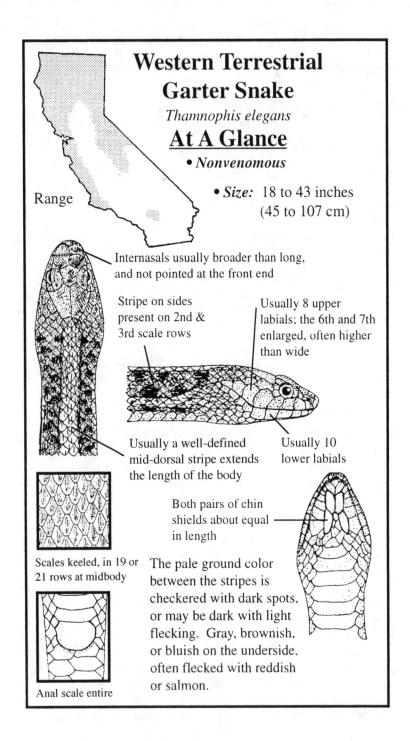

Western Terrestrial Garter Snake

Thamnophis elegans

At A Glance

- *Nonvenomous*

- *Size:* 18 to 43 inches (45 to 107 cm)

Range

Internasals usually broader than long, and not pointed at the front end

Stripe on sides present on 2nd & 3rd scale rows

Usually 8 upper labials; the 6th and 7th enlarged, often higher than wide

Usually a well-defined mid-dorsal stripe extends the length of the body

Usually 10 lower labials

Both pairs of chin shields about equal in length

Scales keeled, in 19 or 21 rows at midbody

The pale ground color between the stripes is checkered with dark spots, or may be dark with light flecking. Gray, brownish, or bluish on the underside, often flecked with reddish or salmon.

Anal scale entire

garter snakes usually have narrow, pointed internasals, and the 6th and 7th upper labials are no longer than they are wide. However, these traits may not necessarily hold true in all areas, and work needs to be done on these snakes.

The northwestern garter snake (24) has 17-17-15 scale rows, 7 upper labials, 8 or 9 lower labials, and a bright yellow, red, or orange dorsal stripe. The Western terrestrial garter snake, where it overlaps with the northwestern, has 19-19-17 or more scale rows, 8 upper labials, 10 lower labials, and usually a dull yellow, brown, or gray dorsal stripe.

The common garter snake (18) has relatively larger eyes, generally 7 upper labials, and usually a plain bluish-gray belly. Where it overlaps with the coast garter snake, it usually has a greenish-yellow dorsal stripe.

Subspecies   Four subspecies are recognized in California.

Klamath Garter Snake

Thamnophis elegans biscutatus
(Cope, 1883)

biscutatus, Latin = two-scaled (pertains to the horizontally divided preocular)

Distinguishing Characteristics   The dorsal and side stripes are separated by a ground color of brown, black, or gray, with obscure spotting. The dorsal stripe is uneven, yellow to brown. This snake is light gray below, often suffused with black or slate, especially on the rear half of the body. The head is rather long and narrow. This snake prefers rocky streams.

Mountain Garter Snake

Thamnophis elegans elegans (Baird & Girard, 1853)

Distinguishing Characteristics   Well-defined stripes on the sides of this subspecies are separated by a velvety black or dark gray-brown ground color. The dorsal stripe is bright yellow, cream, or white, although in some darker specimens it may be reduced to just a trace on the neck. There are no red markings, and the belly is pale with no dark markings. There are light dusky spots or some black coloration down the middle of the belly.

Coast Garter Snake

Thamnophis elegans terrestris (Fox, 1951)

terrestris, Latin = of the earth, terrestrial

Distinguishing Characteristics The dorsal stripe
of this subspecies is typically bright yellow, and the
sides are flecked with bright red or orange spots, even on
the side stripes. This snake usually seeks shelter on land rather than
in water. There is considerable variation in color. In the San Francisco Peninsula area, three yellowish stripes are present, and a checker-
board of black spots occurs between the stripes on a reddish ground
color. In areas along the outer coast from San Mateo County to near
Moss Landing, Monterey County, the dark spots give way to alternating dark and reddish bars on the sides. This color phase also occurs
in the East Bay hills. An increase in dark color, giving almost solid
dark fields between the dorsal and lateral stripes, occurs in the Santa
Cruz Mountains. The mid-dorsal stripe is pale yellow, and the side
stripes are reddish or salmon.

Wandering Garter Snake

Thamnophis elegans vagrans (Baird &
Girard, 1853)

vagrans, Latin = wandering

Distinguishing Characteristics This snake is mostly
brown, greenish, or gray above, with a dull yellow or
brown dorsal stripe fading on the tail and edged with dark
markings that make its border irregular, and which may break the
stripe into dots and dashes. Dark spots on the body are usually small
and well separated and may sometimes be reduced or absent. In
habits, it is either terrestrial or aquatic.

20

Western Aquatic Garter Snake

Culebra de Agua Nómada de Occidente

Thamnophis atratus (Kennicott, 1860)

Thamnos, Greek = a bush, shrub; *ophis,* Greek = snake; *atratus,*
Latin = blackened

Habitat   This species is predominantly aquatic, as its name implies. It is generally found near bodies of water, both standing and flowing, in a variety of habitats.

Prey   As expected in an aquatic snake, prey items include frogs and toads, tadpoles, fish, fish eggs, salamanders, earthworms, and leeches.

Behavior   Behavior of this species is similar to that of other garter snakes. It escapes from predation usually by retreating into water. If caught, it will writhe about and smear its captor with musk and fecal matter and may attempt to bite.

Reproduction   This snake is a live-bearer, producing 7–30 young, about 5 inches (12.7 cm) long, in late summer or early fall.

Similar Species   This snake has pointed internasals (much longer than they are wide), rear chin shields that are noticeably longer than the front pair, and the 6th and 7th upper labials are not greatly enlarged. This will help to separate this species from the Western terrestrial garter snake (19). The common garter snake (18) usually has 7 upper labials, larger eyes, a well-developed dorsal stripe, and distinct red blotches on the sides.

Notes   This species and its subspecies were recently separated from the species *T. couchii* to which they were assigned subspecific status. Rossman, Ford, and Seigel (1996) refer to this species as the Pacific Coast aquatic garter snake, but Western aquatic garter snake has been in use as a common name for many years and seems preferable to me.

Subspecies   Two subspecies of this snake are recognized in California. A third, *T. a. aquaticus,* is now generally considered invalid, and individuals previously assigned to it are now thought to be intergrades between *T. a. atratus* and *T. a. hydrophilus.*

COLUMBRIDS

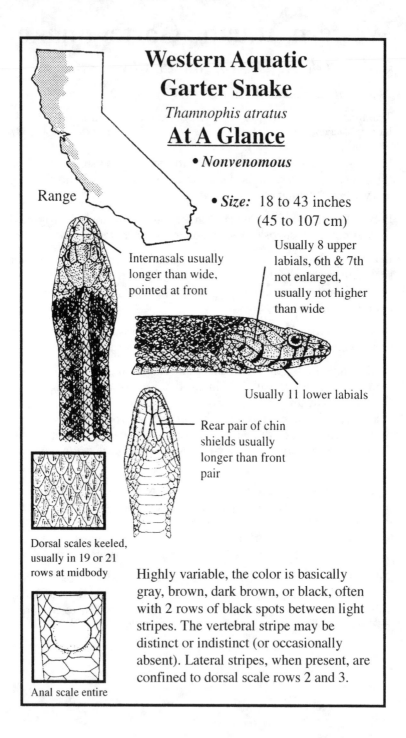

Western Aquatic Garter Snake

Thamnophis atratus

At A Glance

- *Nonvenomous*

Range

- *Size:* 18 to 43 inches (45 to 107 cm)

Internasals usually longer than wide, pointed at front

Usually 8 upper labials, 6th & 7th not enlarged, usually not higher than wide

Usually 11 lower labials

Rear pair of chin shields usually longer than front pair

Dorsal scales keeled, usually in 19 or 21 rows at midbody

Anal scale entire

Highly variable, the color is basically gray, brown, dark brown, or black, often with 2 rows of black spots between light stripes. The vertebral stripe may be distinct or indistinct (or occasionally absent). Lateral stripes, when present, are confined to dorsal scale rows 2 and 3.

Santa Cruz Garter Snake

Thamnophis atratus atratus
(Kennicott, 1860)

Distinguishing Characteristics   This snake has a
yellow-to-orange dorsal stripe, which may be narrow
or wide, more or less conspicuous. Its throat is usually
bright yellow. Its eyes may have a gray or black iris. The snake
may be blotched with salmon or pale yellow on a light blue to green
ground color; but colors and pattern are highly variable. These
snakes have 3 stripes (mid-dorsal orange or yellow-orange stripe and
paler yellowish lateral stripes on each side) throughout most of the
range, but in western Santa Clara, Santa Cruz, San Mateo, and San
Francisco counties, dark pigment obscures the side stripe and the
dorsal stripe is yellowish. South of Monterey Bay, this subspecies and
the Coast subspecies of the Western terrestrial garter snake (19) are
similar in color, but the Santa Cruz garter snake has a deeper yellow
mid-dorsal stripe that is broader in the neck region, a belly that dark-
ens toward the tail, which is often distinctly darker beginning at the
throat; some yellow or orange below; and a yellowish (rather than
whitish) throat and chin.

Oregon Garter Snake

Thamnophis atratus hydrophilus
(Fitch, 1936)

hydro, Greek = water; *philus,* Greek = lover

Distinguishing Characteristics   This subspecies has
conspicuous dark markings in an irregular checkered
arrangement, sometimes blurred by a joining of the spots on a pale
gray ground color. The dorsal stripe is narrow and dull. The lateral
stripes, when present, occur on the 2nd and 3rd dorsal scale rows. It
is light-colored and unmarked below, with a flesh-colored or purplish
tinge toward the tail. It usually has 10 lower labials.

COLUBRIDS

21 Sierra Garter Snake

Culebra de Agua Nómada de Sierra Nevada

Thamnophis couchii (Kennicott, 1859)

Thamnos, Greek = a bush, shrub; *ophis,* Greek = snake; *couchii,* for a Lieutenant Couch of the U. S. Army expedition who obtained the original specimens

Habitat   This is primarily a snake of permanent rivers and rocky streams with protected pools near the shore. It occurs in foothills and into higher mountains to 9,000 feet or more, from north central California to south central California, east of the central valley and into western Nevada. Individuals are occasionally washed down into the Central Valley following spring rains.

Prey   A predominantly aquatic snake, this species eats fish, fish eggs, frogs, toads, salamanders, amphibian larvae, earthworms, and leeches.

Behavior   Similar to the behavior of other garter snakes, this species defends itself in the usual manner and retreats into water when threatened.

Reproduction   Seven to 25 young are born alive in summer and early fall. Young are small, about 5 inches (12.7 cm) long at birth.

Similar Species   The lack of a well-defined dorsal stripe will separate this species from the Western terrestrial garter snake (19); the two-striped garter snake (23) has no mid-dorsal stripe or has only a remnant of a stripe, which appears as a spot on the neck.

Notes   This species once included the two-striped garter snake (23), giant garter snake (22), and the Western aquatic garter snake (20), but recent works have separated these from the Sierra garter snake, leaving it as a distinct species.

Subspecies   There are no subspecies recognized for this snake.

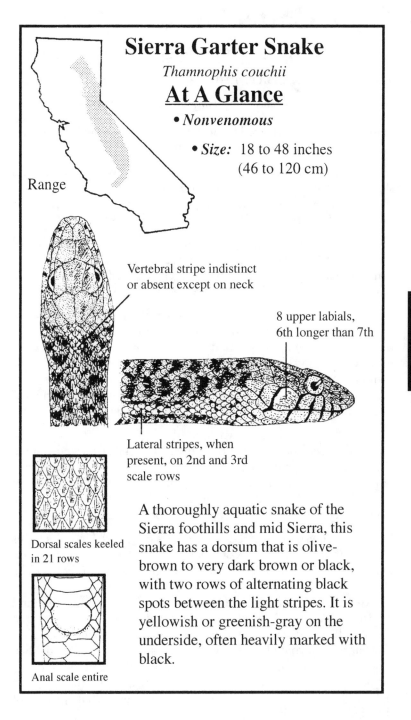

Sierra Garter Snake

Thamnophis couchii

At A Glance

- *Nonvenomous*

- *Size:* 18 to 48 inches
  (46 to 120 cm)

Range

Vertebral stripe indistinct
or absent except on neck

8 upper labials,
6th longer than 7th

Lateral stripes, when
present, on 2nd and 3rd
scale rows

Dorsal scales keeled
in 21 rows

Anal scale entire

A thoroughly aquatic snake of the Sierra foothills and mid Sierra, this snake has a dorsum that is olive-brown to very dark brown or black, with two rows of alternating black spots between the light stripes. It is yellowish or greenish-gray on the underside, often heavily marked with black.

22 Giant Garter Snake

Culebra de Agua Nómada Gigante

Thamnophis gigas Fitch, 1940

Thamnos, Greek = a bush, shrub; *ophis,* Greek = snake; *gigas,* Latin = giant

Status   This snake is listed by both the state and the federal governments under the Endangered Species Act as **THREATENED.**

Habitat   This species is primarily associated with marshes and sloughs, and also irrigation ditches, usually with mud bottoms. It occasionally has been found in slow-moving streams. Emergent plants, such as cattails and tules, are typical basking sites for this snake.

Prey   This snake is thoroughly aquatic and feeds on fish and amphibians (including introduced species such as carp, mosquito fish, and bullfrogs, since these have largely replaced native Sacramento blackfish, thick-tailed chub, and red-legged frogs).

Behavior   This snake essentially occupies the niche filled by some water snakes (genus *Nerodia*) in the eastern United States, being thoroughly aquatic (rarely found away from the water) and foraging in water for food. It basks on willow, saltbush, or tule mats and is extremely wary, dropping into the water or into dense vegetation at the slightest disturbance. Occasionally it will bask in higher shrubs or trees, which are situated over the water, so it can dive in at any alarm.

Reproduction   Little is known about the reproductive history of this snake in the wild, and because of its threatened status, it is uncommon to nonexistent in captive collections. It is live bearing and probably gives birth to 10–46 young in late summer or early fall. Newborns range from 7.9–12 inches (20–30.6 cm) and grow rapidly. They may reach sexual maturity in three or more years, but this is not definitely known.

Notes   Formerly considered a subspecies of *T. couchii,* this species was elevated to full species status when it was not found to intergrade with *T. couchii* or *T. atratus,* to which it had been shown to be closely related biochemically.

Extensive modification of the Central Valley for farming and industry has greatly reduced this snake's range. With the damming of the Kern River in 1952, feeding what was once Lake Buena Vista, it is now largely extirpated in the central and southern parts of the San Joaquin Valley. Its adaptation to mud-bottomed irrigation ditches in the Sacramento Valley farther north is a saving grace for it.

Subspecies   Currently there are no recognized subspecies of this snake.

Giant Garter Snake
Thamnophis gigas
<u>At A Glance</u>
- *Nonvenomous*
- *Size:* 18 to 64 inches (46 to 160 cm)
- *Threatened Species (California)*

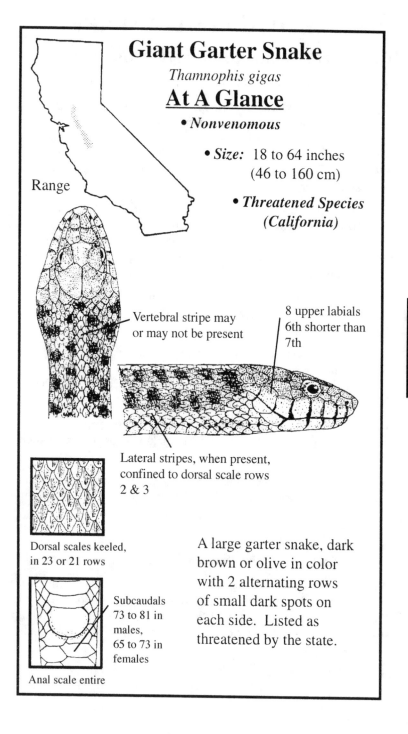

Range

COLUBRIDS

Vertebral stripe may or may not be present

8 upper labials 6th shorter than 7th

Lateral stripes, when present, confined to dorsal scale rows 2 & 3

Dorsal scales keeled, in 23 or 21 rows

Subcaudals 73 to 81 in males, 65 to 73 in females

Anal scale entire

A large garter snake, dark brown or olive in color with 2 alternating rows of small dark spots on each side. Listed as threatened by the state.

23 Two-striped Garter Snake

Culebra de Agua Nómada de Dos-rayadas

Thamnophis hammondii (Kennicott, 1860)

Thamnos, Greek = a bush, shrub; *ophis,* Greek = snake; *hammondii,* for W. A. Hammond, collector of the original specimen

Status This species is considered a federal species of concern. It is **PROTECTED** by state law and may not be taken or possessed without a special permit.

Habitat This snake is found in or near permanent fresh water, often along pools in streams with rocky beds bordered by willow or other streamside vegetation. It is one of the most aquatic of the garter snakes, found in oak woodland, mixed oak, and chaparral environments, along with pastures and fields, as long as water is present.

Prey The two-striped garter snake is almost exclusively aquatic in its foraging, eating tadpoles, frogs and toads, fish, and fish eggs. Earthworms are also said to be eaten.

Behavior This snake is often active at dusk or at night, but it may be encountered in the daytime. When captured, it will writhe about and smear its captor with feces and musk, and occasionally will bite. It usually takes to water at the slightest disturbance.

Reproduction Live-bearing, with 16–25 young produced in late summer through mid-fall. Newborn snakes measure 8–8.7 inches (20.3–21.7 cm) in length.

Similar Species Three other species of garter snakes: the common (18), Western terrestrial (19), and Western aquatic (20) all have mid-dorsal stripes, at least in areas where their range overlaps that of the two-striped garter snake. In the vicinity of Mt. Pinos and Frazier Mountain, its range may abut or even overlap to some extent that of the Sierra garter snake (21), to which it is closely related and resembles.

Notes Loss of wetland habitats in southern California is the primary cause of its decline, as it is with many aquatic or riparian species in this region. Other problems may be the disappearance of amphibians (food source), water pollution, and the fact that it is just plain killed by many people.

Subspecies There are no recognized subspecies of this snake.

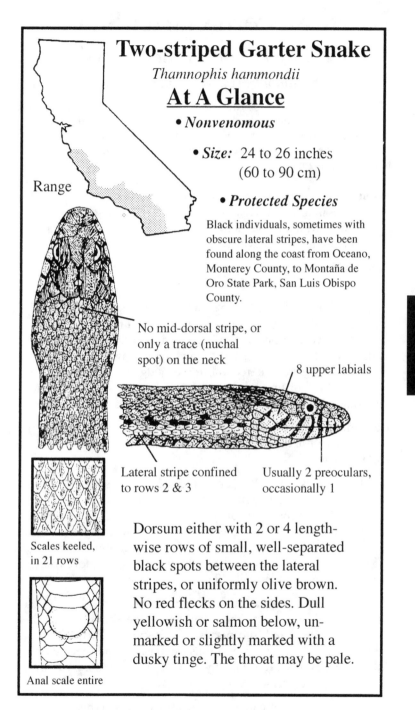

Two-striped Garter Snake
Thamnophis hammondii
At A Glance

• *Nonvenomous*

• *Size:* 24 to 26 inches (60 to 90 cm)

• *Protected Species*

Range

Black individuals, sometimes with obscure lateral stripes, have been found along the coast from Oceano, Monterey County, to Montaña de Oro State Park, San Luis Obispo County.

No mid-dorsal stripe, or only a trace (nuchal spot) on the neck

8 upper labials

Lateral stripe confined to rows 2 & 3

Usually 2 preoculars, occasionally 1

Scales keeled, in 21 rows

Dorsum either with 2 or 4 lengthwise rows of small, well-separated black spots between the lateral stripes, or uniformly olive brown. No red flecks on the sides. Dull yellowish or salmon below, unmarked or slightly marked with a dusky tinge. The throat may be pale.

Anal scale entire

24 Northwestern Garter Snake

Culebra de Agua Nómada del Noroeste

Thamnophis ordinoides (Baird & Girard, 1852)

Thamnos, Greek = a bush, shrub; *ophis,* Greek = snake; *ordinoides* = Baird & Girard observed longitudinal rows of black spots between the stripes of their specimens. These spots reminded them of *Tropidonotus ordinatus* (= *Thamnophis s. sirtalis*), and they apparently intended the name ordinoides to mean "ordinatus-like."

Habitat   This garter snake is chiefly terrestrial, frequenting meadows or clearings in forested areas where there is abundant low vegetation. It is associated with the coastal fog belt. Although it has been seen swimming, it is less associated with water than most other garter snakes.

Prey   This species consumes slugs and earthworms, although occasionally it will eat salamanders and frogs.

Behavior   This snake is most active on warm, sunny days, although it is frequently about in cooler weather. When frightened, it usually seeks dense vegetation. Depending upon its color phase, its reaction to danger differs: Striped snakes crawl directly away because it is difficult for predators to detect motion or judge the speed of a striped object; spotted or unmarked snakes suddenly change direction and then stay still, essentially camouflaging themselves from predators.

Reproduction   Live bearing, with 3–20 (average 8–12) young born from June to August. Newborns measure about 6–7.5 inches (15–19 cm) in length.

Similar Species   The Western terrestrial garter snake (19) usually has 8 upper labials and a higher dorsal scale row count. The Oregon garter snake, a subspecies of the Western aquatic garter snake (20) found in the same range, generally has a narrow, dull yellow, brown, or gray dorsal stripe and 8 upper labials. The common garter snake (18) lacks red markings on the belly; has a longer, more triangular head; larger eyes; and usually 19 scale rows at midbody.

Notes   This was once a "catchall" species and nearly all of the garter snakes in California, with the exception of the common and checkered, were considered "subspecies" of this species. Further study illuminated the relationships, and thus established one species with no subspecies. Even so, it is a highly variable snake with a great array of colors and patterns.

Subspecies   There are no recognized subspecies of this snake.

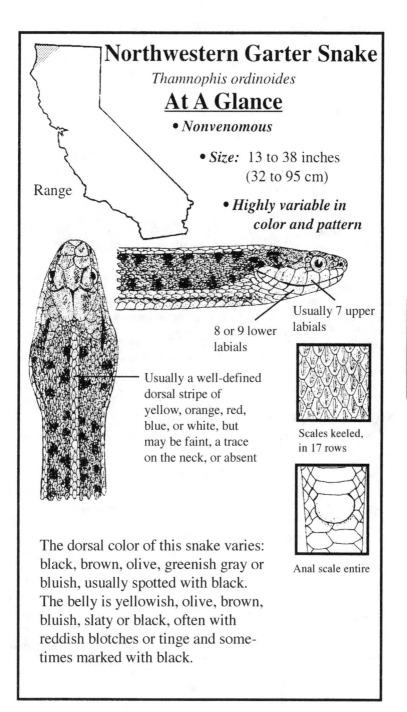

Northwestern Garter Snake

Thamnophis ordinoides

At A Glance

- *Nonvenomous*

- *Size:* 13 to 38 inches (32 to 95 cm)

- *Highly variable in color and pattern*

Range

Usually 7 upper labials

8 or 9 lower labials

Usually a well-defined dorsal stripe of yellow, orange, red, blue, or white, but may be faint, a trace on the neck, or absent

Scales keeled, in 17 rows

Anal scale entire

The dorsal color of this snake varies: black, brown, olive, greenish gray or bluish, usually spotted with black. The belly is yellowish, olive, brown, bluish, slaty or black, often with reddish blotches or tinge and sometimes marked with black.

25 Checkered Garter Snake

Sochuate

Thamnophis marcianus (Baird & Girard, 1853)

Thamnos, Greek = a bush, shrub; ophis, Greek = snake; marcianus, named for Marcy

Habitat   This species is found in arid grasslands and deserts, although apparently never far from some source of water. In California, it is mostly associated with the Colorado River and associated irrigation canals.

Prey   As aggressive, largely terrestrial predators, these snakes have been known to consume slugs, earthworms, crayfish, fish, frogs, toads, salamanders, lizards, and small mammals, as well as carrion.

Behavior   Little is known about the behavior of this snake. It appears to forage primarily at night, at least in the warmer times of the year. They forage around the edges of ponds and even in roadways.

Reproduction   Like other garter snakes, this species is live-bearing, with 4–18 (average 12.8) young born from June through August. The young measure 7–9.25 inches (17.7–23.5 cm) in length.

Similar Species   No other garter snakes occur within this same range.

Notes   This snake is quickly disappearing throughout much of its range because of human use of water sources for agriculture and degradation of habitat.

Subspecies   One subspecies of this snake occurs in California.

Marcy's Checkered Garter Snake

Thamnophis marcianus marcianus
(Baird & Girard, 1853)

Distinguishing Characteristics   This is the only sub-species of this snake that occurs in the United States (two others occur in Mexico and Central America). It has a large range that extends from eastern California to central Texas, southwestern Kansas to northern Mexico.

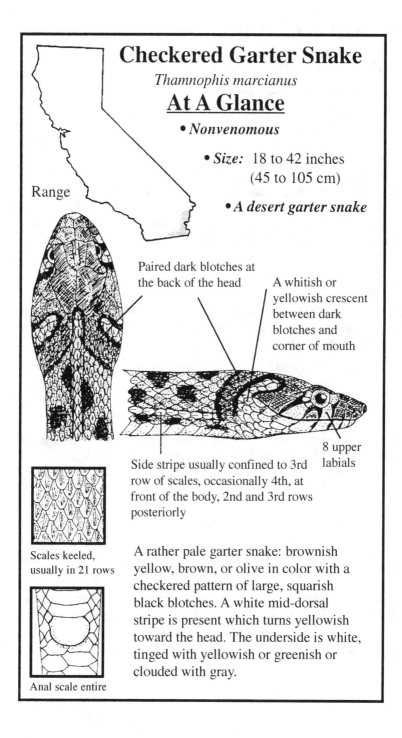

Checkered Garter Snake

Thamnophis marcianus

At A Glance

• *Nonvenomous*

• *Size:* 18 to 42 inches (45 to 105 cm)

• *A desert garter snake*

Range

Paired dark blotches at the back of the head

A whitish or yellowish crescent between dark blotches and corner of mouth

8 upper labials

Side stripe usually confined to 3rd row of scales, occasionally 4th, at front of the body, 2nd and 3rd rows posteriorly

Scales keeled, usually in 21 rows

Anal scale entire

A rather pale garter snake: brownish yellow, brown, or olive in color with a checkered pattern of large, squarish black blotches. A white mid-dorsal stripe is present which turns yellowish toward the head. The underside is white, tinged with yellowish or greenish or clouded with gray.

COLUBRIDS

26 Ground Snake

Culebra de Arena (Culebra de Tierra)

Sonora semiannulata Baird & Girard, 1853

semiannulata, Latin = half-ringed (in reference to the body crossbands that fail to cross the venter)

Habitat This snake can be found in almost any semi-arid area with hiding places, including deserts, wooded rocky terrain, prairies, piñon-juniper woodlands, and limestone embankments. In California, this species is found in sandy or gravelly desert regions that have some subsurface water. They favor riverbottoms. Along the lower Colorado River, this snake inhabits mesquite, arrowweed, and willow thickets.

Prey The ground snake feeds primarily on small invertebrates, such as spiders, scorpions, centipedes, crickets, grasshoppers, and insect larvae. Shallow grooves on the outer sides of the rear teeth suggest that these snakes may be venomous (Stebbins, 1985), but they are not dangerous to humans.

Behavior This snake is not rare, and, in fact, may be one of the most common snakes in western North America (Rossi and Rossi, 1994). However, it is very secretive and is seldom seen. It is an adept burrower and also hides in rock crevices. It is nocturnal in habits.

Reproduction *Sonora* is oviparous, laying eggs from May through July. The eggs hatch in 53–67 days, and young are 2.75–5 inches (7–12.5 cm) long. Little is known about the reproductive history of this species. It is seldom kept in captivity due to its secretive and nocturnal habits.

Similar Species The Western shovelnose snake (27) has dark crossbands, a flatter snout, and a deeply inset lower jaw. Black-headed snakes (28, 29) have dark heads, no crossbands, and no loreal scale.

Notes This snake, which is highly variable in color and pattern, has been misdescribed as several separate species over the years. Now it is recognized as a single species. Several color and pattern combinations can emerge from a single clutch of eggs!

Subspecies There are no recognized subspecies of this snake.

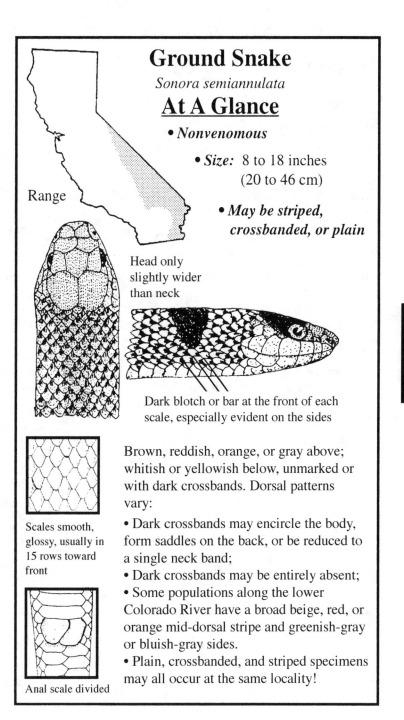

Ground Snake
Sonora semiannulata
At A Glance

- *Nonvenomous*
- *Size:* 8 to 18 inches (20 to 46 cm)
- *May be striped, crossbanded, or plain*

Range

Head only slightly wider than neck

Dark blotch or bar at the front of each scale, especially evident on the sides

Scales smooth, glossy, usually in 15 rows toward front

Anal scale divided

Brown, reddish, orange, or gray above; whitish or yellowish below, unmarked or with dark crossbands. Dorsal patterns vary:

- Dark crossbands may encircle the body, form saddles on the back, or be reduced to a single neck band;
- Dark crossbands may be entirely absent;
- Some populations along the lower Colorado River have a broad beige, red, or orange mid-dorsal stripe and greenish-gray or bluish-gray sides.
- Plain, crossbanded, and striped specimens may all occur at the same locality!

COLUBRIDS

27 Western Shovelnose Snake

(Western Shovel-nosed Snake)

Culebra Palanaria Occidental

Chionactis occipitalis (Hallowell, 1854)

Chioneos, Greek = bright, white as snow; *aktis,* Greek = a ray, beam

Habitat The shovelnose snake is a sand swimmer—a burrower that moves about just below the surface of loose sand in desert regions. It is found in areas of sparse vegetation.

Prey This snake is primarily insectivorous, eating insects and their larval stages, spiders, scorpions, centipedes, and buried moth pupae.

Behavior This nocturnally active species emerges after dark to pursue its insect prey. There are a few records of daytime activity, usually on cooler days. It reaches its peak of activity in May and June. It moves through the sand with a lateral, undulatory motion, leaving a sinuous track with sand piled up in the rear margin of each side loop. During movement, the ventral scales are drawn in through the action of abdominal muscles, forming a concave undersurface, which may aid them in moving across loose sand. When moving across an uncomfortable substrate or when frightened, they may move in a sidewinding motion.

Reproduction Shovelnose snakes are oviparous, and they lay 2–4 (perhaps as many as 9) eggs, which measure about 5 by 14 mm. Young snakes are 4–5 inches (10–13 cm) long at hatching.

Similar Species The ground snake (26) has dark pigment at the base of most dorsal scales, and the snout is not as obviously flattened.

Notes This snake is sometimes docile, but usually it is pugnacious, striking repeatedly at moving objects within their range. They are too small to effectively bite humans. Some real fighters may even "leap" off the ground with the force of their strike!

Subspecies Three subspecies are recognized in California.

Western Shovelnose Snake

Chionactis occipitalis

At A Glance

• *Nonvenomous*

• *Size:* 10 to 17 inches (25 to 42 cm)

• *A dark-and-light banded snake*

Range

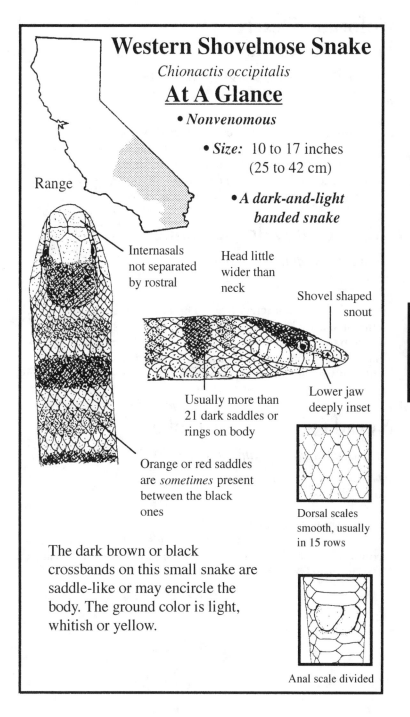

Internasals not separated by rostral

Head little wider than neck

Shovel shaped snout

Usually more than 21 dark saddles or rings on body

Lower jaw deeply inset

Orange or red saddles are *sometimes* present between the black ones

Dorsal scales smooth, usually in 15 rows

The dark brown or black crossbands on this small snake are saddle-like or may encircle the body. The ground color is light, whitish or yellow.

Anal scale divided

Colorado Desert Shovelnose Snake

Chionactis occipitalis annulata (Baird, 1859)

annulata, Latin = ringed

Distinguishing Characteristics   The crossbands on this form are usually black. There are usually fewer than 45 bands across the body, plus the unmarked front band positions on the lower surface (indicated by the ends of the dorsal bands). Narrow red crossbands are present between the black bands.

Mojave Shovelnose Snake

Chionactis occipitalis occipitalis
(Hallowell, 1854)

Distinguishing Characteristics   The crossbands on this snake are brown with no black or brown secondary bands between the primary ones. There are usually 45 or more bands on the body, plus the unmarked front band positions on the lower surface. No narrow red crossbands are present.

Nevada Shovelnose Snake

Chionactis occipitalis talpina Klauber, 1951

talpa, Latin = a mole; *-ina,* Latin = likeness, derived from

Distinguishing Characteristics   Dark scales are present in the spaces between the broad bands and may form secondary bands. There are usually 152 or more ventrals in males and 160 or more in females.

28 Western Black-headed Snake

Culebra Cabeza Negra Occidental

Tantilla planiceps (Blainville, 1835)

Tantillum, Latin = so small a thing (a reference to the small size of these snakes); *planus,* Latin = flat, *caput,* Latin = head

Habitat   This small snake has been found in chaparral, grassland, and oak woodland environments and the desert's edge. It is found under stones, logs, boards, or plant debris on both hillsides and on level ground, and otherwise spends time underground in crevices or animal burrows. In arid lands, it occurs along rocky edges of washes, arroyos, and streams, and on rocky hillsides.

Prey   This snake is insectivorous and eats mainly beetle larvae and centipedes.

Behavior   Little is known about this species. It appears to be crepuscular and nocturnal, and it is found abroad only at night, occasionally on roads. Up to six individuals have been found together under surface objects.

Reproduction   Almost nothing is known about the reproductive history of this species. It is an egg-layer. Up to four eggs were found in a female snake's body. Presumably copulation occurs in spring with the eggs laid in summer.

Similar Species   In the Southwestern black-headed snake (29), the black cap usually does not extend below the corner of the mouth, and there are no dark spots bordering the pale collar.

Notes   The black-headed and flat-headed snakes (genus *Tantilla*) are a widespread group of species found throughout much of the southern half of the United States, yet not much is known about them. Identification of species is often accomplished by looking at the structure of the hemipenes (the male copulatory organ). The distribution of the various species is often spotty, and their environmental needs are unknown. These are snakes with a great potential for study.

Subspecies   There are no currently recognized subspecies of this snake.

COLUBRIDS

Western Black-headed Snake

Tantilla planiceps
At A Glance

• *Mildly Venomous*

• *Size:* 5 to 15.5 inches (13 to 39 cm)

Range

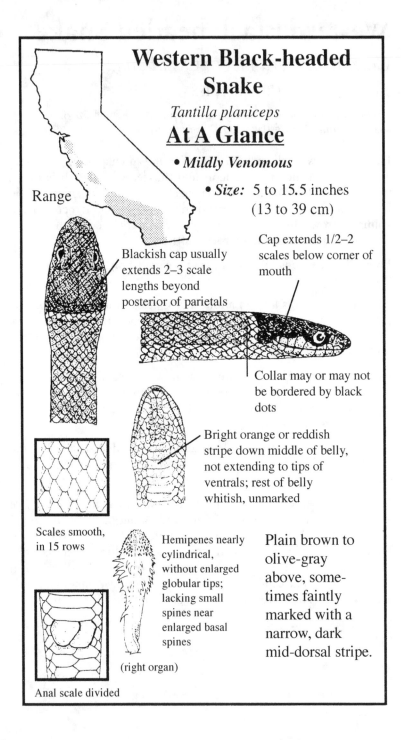

Blackish cap usually extends 2–3 scale lengths beyond posterior of parietals

Cap extends 1/2–2 scales below corner of mouth

Collar may or may not be bordered by black dots

Bright orange or reddish stripe down middle of belly, not extending to tips of ventrals; rest of belly whitish, unmarked

Scales smooth, in 15 rows

Hemipenes nearly cylindrical, without enlarged globular tips; lacking small spines near enlarged basal spines

(right organ)

Anal scale divided

Plain brown to olive-gray above, sometimes faintly marked with a narrow, dark mid-dorsal stripe.

Southwestern
Black-headed Snake

Culebra Cabeza Negra del Suroeste

Tantilla hobartsmithi Taylor, 1936

Tantillum, Latin = so small a thing (a reference to the small size of these snakes); *hobartsmithi,* honoring Dr. Hobart M. Smith, herpetologist at the University of Colorado

Habitat   This snake inhabits brushland, grassland, creosote bush, chaparral, and piñon-juniper woodland environments and open coniferous forests in the Sierra foothills and Great Basin region. It is attracted to stream courses and canyon bottoms. By day, it hides under rocks, logs, boards, dead *Yucca,* or other plant debris.

Prey   This snake eats invertebrates—millipedes, centipedes, and insects such as beetle larvae and caterpillars.

Behavior   Very little observation of this species has been done. It is apparently crepuscular to nocturnal.

Reproduction   Again, we know very little. A clutch of presumably 1–3 eggs is laid in June or July, possibly August.

Similar Species   See the Western black-headed snake (28).

Notes   Populations of this species in California were previously known as *Tantilla utahensis.* Much study still needs to be done on the systematics of this group.

Black-headed snakes are "rear fanged." The slightly enlarged, grooved teeth in the back of the jaw are thought to aid in injecting venom (not dangerous to a human, even if this snake was big enough to bite one) into their prey.

Subspecies   There are no described subspecies for this snake.

COLUBRIDS

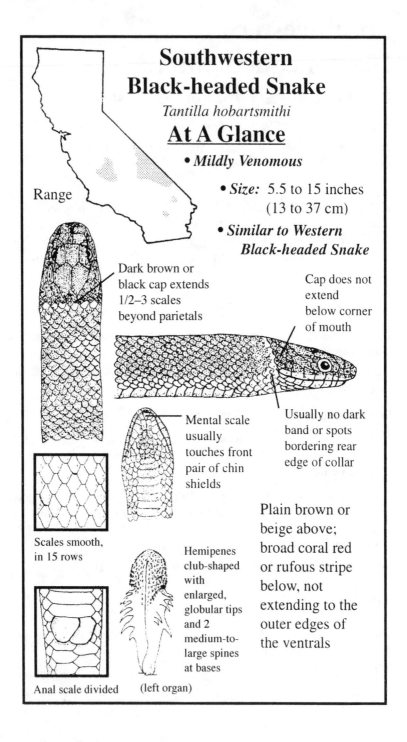

Southwestern Black-headed Snake

Tantilla hobartsmithi

At A Glance

- *Mildly Venomous*
- *Size:* 5.5 to 15 inches (13 to 37 cm)
- *Similar to Western Black-headed Snake*

Range

Dark brown or black cap extends 1/2–3 scales beyond parietals

Cap does not extend below corner of mouth

Mental scale usually touches front pair of chin shields

Usually no dark band or spots bordering rear edge of collar

Scales smooth, in 15 rows

Hemipenes club-shaped with enlarged, globular tips and 2 medium-to-large spines at bases

Plain brown or beige above; broad coral red or rufous stripe below, not extending to the outer edges of the ventrals

Anal scale divided

(left organ)

³⁰ Lyre Snake

Codorniz

Trimorphodon biscutatus (Duméril, Bibron & Duméril, 1854)

Trimorphodon, Latin = three tooth shapes (refers to the three tooth shapes in the upper jaw; long, recurved anterior teeth, shorter middle teeth, and the long, grooved fangs at the rear); *biscutatus,* Latin = two scales (probably refers to the doubled loreal scale)

Habitat   This is a snake of rocky regions, found in rocky canyons and hillsides throughout habitats such as chaparral, piñon-juniper woodland, desert grassland, desert creosote-bush scrub, oak woodland, and coastal sage scrub. Although occasionally found in rockless areas, it prefers areas that contain large boulders with deep fissures in which it seeks refuge during the day. It has been found from sea level to 7,400 feet (Shaw and Campbell, 1974).

Prey   The lyre snake eats lizards, especially crevice-dwellers such as night lizards and geckos, and small mammals, including bats, which are caught at their roosting sites. They also reportedly eat small birds and other snakes. They immobilize prey by injecting a mild venom with their enlarged, grooved teeth located at the rear of the jaw. Sometimes they constrict the prey.

Behavior   Lyre snakes are nocturnal, although they may also be active within deep rock crevices in the early morning hours. They have been found abroad at every month of the year except November and in temperatures as low as 64°F (17.7°C) (Stebbins, 1954). When confronted, the lyre snake may raise the front portion of its body and strike at its tormentor. It will also, like many other snakes, vibrate its tail when in a defensive coil.

Reproduction   Oviparous, the lyre snake lays 7–20 eggs from June to September after mating from March to May. After an incubation period of 77–79 days, hatchlings emerge at a length of 8–9 inches (20–23 cm).

Similar Species   Gopher snakes (14) and the glossy snake (13) have round pupils and a broad neck.

Notes   The lyre snake is perhaps the only mildly venomous snake that is large enough to bite a human. Studies suggest that the venom is somewhat hemorrhagic (blood-destroying) in nature, but its effects on humans are little known. However, most people who have been bitten (including the author) report localized swelling, itching, and

COLUBRIDS

Lyre Snake
Trimorphodon biscutatus
At A Glance

• *Mildly Venomous*

 • *Size:* 18 to 47.8 inches
 (45 to 121 cm)

 • *A "cat-eyed" snake*

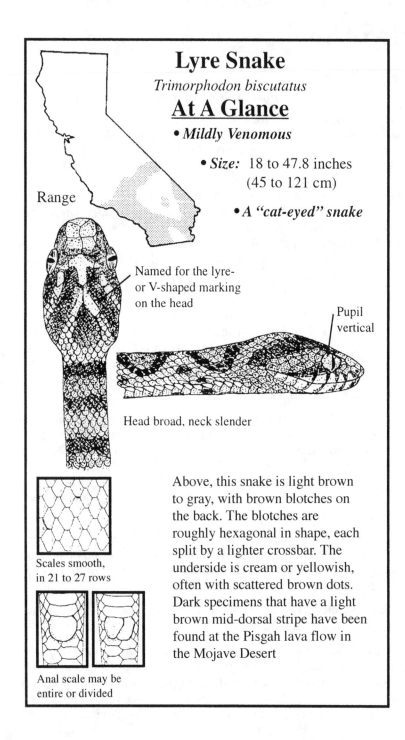

Range

Named for the lyre-
or V-shaped marking
on the head

Pupil
vertical

Head broad, neck slender

Scales smooth,
in 21 to 27 rows

Anal scale may be
entire or divided

Above, this snake is light brown
to gray, with brown blotches on
the back. The blotches are
roughly hexagonal in shape, each
split by a lighter crossbar. The
underside is cream or yellowish,
often with scattered brown dots.
Dark specimens that have a light
brown mid-dorsal stripe have been
found at the Pisgah lava flow in
the Mojave Desert

redness. The snake needs to chew for a considerable period to work the venom into a wound, and most people will not permit a snake to continue biting them for an extended period.

Subspecies   Two subspecies of the lyre snake occur in California.

Sonoran Lyre Snake

Trimorphodon biscutatus lambda
Cope, 1886

lambda, Greek = chevron (referring to the shape of the head markings)

Distinguishing Characteristics   The lyre-shaped or chevron-shaped marking on the head is quite distinct in this subspecies. It has 34 or fewer (average 28) dorsal blotches. The anal scale is divided.

California Lyre Snake

Trimorphodon biscutatus vandenburghi
Klauber, 1924

vandenburghi, honoring John Van Denburgh (1872-1924), eminent herpetologist at the California Academy of Sciences

Distinguishing Characteristics   This subspecies also has a distinct V-shaped marking (closed end of the V forward) on the head, and it has 28 to 43 (average 35) dorsal blotches. The anal scale is usually entire (undivided).

Night Snake

Culebra Nocturna

Hypsiglena torquata (Günther, 1860)

Hypsos, Greek = high; *glenes,* Greek = the eyeball, something to stare at; *torquata,* Latin = adorned with a necklace

Habitat   Night snakes are found in many habitats, including sage-brush flats, desert scrub, grassland, chaparral, riparian, and oak woodland areas, and even moist mountain meadows. They are found from sea level to 8,700 feet (Shaw and Campbell, 1974) and, like lyre snakes, seem to prefer rocky areas within the habitat.

Prey   The night snake eats lizards, small snakes (especially blind snakes), small frogs, tadpoles, slender salamanders, and small fish (McKeown, 1997). It also consumes small toads and probably insects (Stebbins, 1954), centipedes, scorpions, and reptile eggs (Rossi and Rossi, 1994). In captivity, it will also accept small mammals such as "pinky" (newborn) mice. Prey is immobilized with venom that is worked into the bite by means of enlarged teeth at the back of the upper jaw.

Behavior   The night snake, as its name implies, is active at dusk and at night. During the day it can be found under rocks, logs or other surface objects, or in rock crevices. It sometimes hibernates in burrows dug by desert tortoises (Shaw and Campbell, 1974).

Reproduction   The night snake is an egg-layer, laying 3 or 4 eggs from April to June. These eggs hatch anywhere from 47–52 days later (Rossi and Rossi, 1994). The eggs measure 9–11 mm by 22–32 mm. Hatchlings emerge at a length of 6.7 inches (17 cm).

Similar Species   The lyre snake (30) has pale crossbars within its dorsal blotches, and usually has a V-shaped marking on the top of the head. The glossy snake (13) has a single anal plate and more rounded pupils. A juvenile racer (7) has round pupils and a lower preocular scale wedged between its upper labials. Young gopher snakes (14) have rounded eye pupils and usually 4 prefrontal scales. Young rattlesnakes (33 - 38) have a horny button or rattle at the end of the tail.

Notes   Although mildly venomous, the night snake seldom attempts to bite, and few specimens are large enough to pose a threat to humans. There is little information on the effects of bites to humans, but it is probably very minor.

Subspecies   Three subspecies of night snake occur in California.

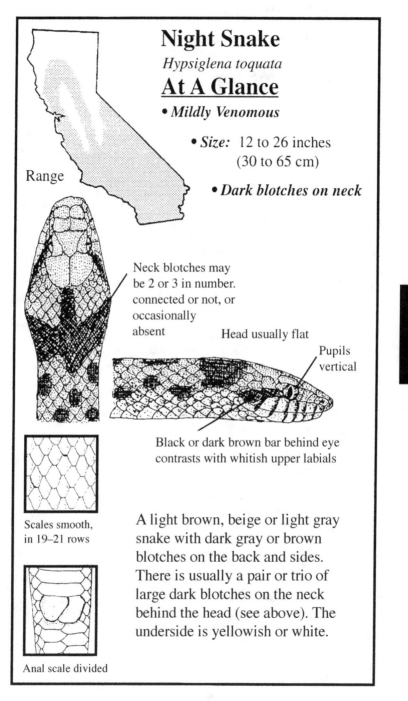

Night Snake
Hypsiglena toquata
At A Glance

• *Mildly Venomous*

• *Size:* 12 to 26 inches
(30 to 65 cm)

• *Dark blotches on neck*

Range

Neck blotches may
be 2 or 3 in number.
connected or not, or
occasionally
absent

Head usually flat

Pupils
vertical

Black or dark brown bar behind eye
contrasts with whitish upper labials

Scales smooth,
in 19–21 rows

Anal scale divided

A light brown, beige or light gray
snake with dark gray or brown
blotches on the back and sides.
There is usually a pair or trio of
large dark blotches on the neck
behind the head (see above). The
underside is yellowish or white.

COLUBRIDS

Desert Night Snake

Hypsiglena torquata deserticola
Tanner, 1944

deserere, Latin = to desert or abandon; *cola,* Latin =
inhabitant (a reference to this subspecies' occurrence in
desert regions)

Distinguishing Characteristics   The large spots on the
neck of this subspecies are greatly enlarged, covering nearly all of
the nape and contacting the parietals or the scales immediately
behind the parietals.

San Diego Night Snake

Hypsiglena torquata klauberi Tanner, 1944

klauberi, honoring Laurence M. Klauber (1883-1968)
of San Diego, eminent herpetologist and student of
western reptiles

Distinguishing Characteristics   This subspecies has
dorsal scales in 21 rows at the 100th ventral. It has 8 upper
labials, a single loreal scale, and usually 3 large spots on the neck.

California Night Snake

Hypsiglena torquata nuchalata Tanner, 1943

nuchalis, Latin = of the neck; *-atus,*
Latin = provided with

Distinguishing Characteristics   The dorsal scales
are in 19 rows at the 100th ventral, and there are usually 7
upper labials.

Family Hydrophiidae: Sea Snakes

This family contains about 50 species of snakes which live in the ocean and feed primarily upon fish. All sea snakes are venomous and have short, immovable hollow fangs at the front of the mouth. They are closely related to the family Elapidae, which includes snakes such as coral snakes and cobras; in fact, some authorities consider sea snakes a subfamily of the elapids.

Sea snakes generally grow to 2–4 feet in length, although a few may get to be as long as 9 feet. They are highly adapted to marine life, having laterally flattened bodies and expanded, oarlike tails. Most sea snakes are live-bearing and have their young in rocky pools near shore, on shore, or in the open ocean. A few that lay eggs must come ashore to lay them.

Sea snakes are widespread in tropical and subtropical seas, but do not occur in the Atlantic Ocean.

32 Yellowbelly Sea Snake

Víbora del Mar

Pelamis platurus (Linnaeus, 1766)

Pelamis, Greek (apparently obsolete) = a young tuna; *platys*, Greek = flat; *oura*, Greek = tail

Habitat   This sea snake has the largest range of any serpent in the world, found in the Pacific and Indian Oceans from the coasts of Africa, Asia, and Australia to southern Siberia, the Pacific Coast,

Figure 4. Yellowbelly sea snake

including Central America and Mexico, and the mid-Pacific around the Hawaiian Islands. It ranges into the Gulf of California (Sea of Cortez) and along the Pacific Coast of Baja California. It has been reported in southern California waters from the San Diego area and as far north as San Clemente in Orange County (Stebbins, 1985). These sightings probably coincide with "El Niño" events in which warmer waters move into the normally cooler waters off the Pacific Coast every few years.

Prey   The sea snake primarily eats fish, including eels, which it immobilizes with its highly toxic venom.

Behavior   The yellowbelly sea snake is a very good swimmer and diver, and although it is attracted to shallow offshore waters, it may also be found far out at sea. It frequents slicks, areas where currents converge and rafts of seaweed, driftwood, and other debris collect. These floating masses attract small fish, upon which the snake feeds, and sometimes protect the snake from other predators. Although graceful and agile in water, this snake is nearly helpless on land.

Reproduction   The yellowbelly sea snake is a live-bearer, having 1–8 young, perhaps throughout the year.

Similar Species   No other sea snakes occur in California, and the bright colors and contrasting pattern, along with the paddle-like tail, make this species easily distinguished from any other snake. Eels, which are fish, lack distinct scalation.

Notes   Although the venom of the yellowbelly sea snake is very potent, the snake is not aggressive toward humans and not inclined to bite. There have been few human fatalities, and when humans are bitten, venom seldom appears to be injected (Stebbins, 1985).

Subspecies   There are no recognized subspecies of this snake.

Yellowbelly Sea Snake

Pelamis platurus

At A Glance

- *Venomous*

  - *Size:* 20 to 45 inches (50 to 113 cm)

  - *An open ocean-dwelling snake, highly adapted to a marine existence*

Range

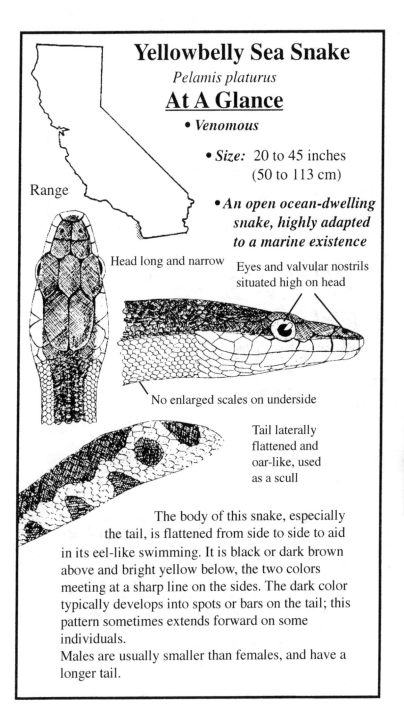

Head long and narrow

Eyes and valvular nostrils situated high on head

No enlarged scales on underside

Tail laterally flattened and oar-like, used as a scull

The body of this snake, especially the tail, is flattened from side to side to aid in its eel-like swimming. It is black or dark brown above and bright yellow below, the two colors meeting at a sharp line on the sides. The dark color typically develops into spots or bars on the tail; this pattern sometimes extends forward on some individuals.

Males are usually smaller than females, and have a longer tail.

Family Viperidae: Vipers
Subfamily Crotalinae: Pit Vipers

This subfamily (considered a full family by many herpetologists) includes, in the United States, the rattlesnakes, copperheads, and water moccasins (cottonmouths). Worldwide, it contains about 125 species with members in Europe, Asia, and Africa, as well as throughout the Americas. In California, only rattlesnakes represent this group.

The venom-injecting mechanism of these snakes is the most highly advanced of any venomous snake. Large, movable hollow fangs are located at the front of the upper jaw. At rest, the fangs are folded up toward the roof of the mouth. The snake swings the fangs forward when biting so that the victim may be stabbed in a sudden thrust.

Pit vipers are so called because of a specialized pit in the loreal scale on each side of the face. This opens into a very sensitive structure that allows them to detect the body heat of endothermic ("warm-blooded") prey and to strike accurately.

RATTLESNAKE HEAD SCALES

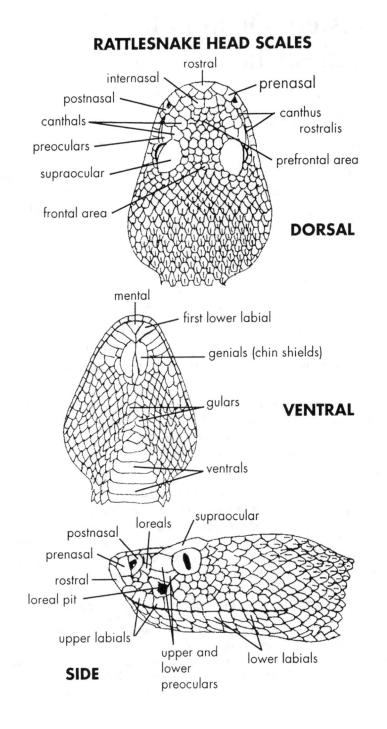

rostral

internasal

prenasal

postnasal

canthus
rostralis

canthals

preoculars

prefrontal area

supraocular

frontal area

DORSAL

mental

first lower labial

genials (chin shields)

gulars

VENTRAL

ventrals

loreals

supraocular

postnasal

prenasal

rostral

loreal pit

upper labials

upper and
lower
preoculars

lower labials

SIDE

33 Western Diamondback Rattlesnake

Víbora Serrana

Crotalus atrox Baird & Girard, 1853

krotalon, Greek = a little bell, a rattle; *atrox*, Latin = fearful, cruel

Habitat   The Western diamondback rattlesnake occurs in a variety of arid and semi-arid habitats, including open desert, grassland, shrubland, and woodland environments. In California, it is found almost entirely in desert regions, including both open desert and rocky canyons and hillsides.

Prey   This large rattlesnake eats rabbits, rodents (rats, mice, squirrels, etc.), birds, and lizards.

Behavior   This snake is most active at dusk and at night, particularly during the hotter times of the year. In spring and on cooler days, it may be abroad in the daytime. It is prone to stand its ground when confronted and, because of its size, boldness, and large amount of potent venom, it is considered one of the most dangerous snakes in the country.

Reproduction   Mating occurs in spring (as early as March 25) (Stebbins, 1954) and occasionally in the fall. Young are born alive in late summer or fall. The number of young ranges from 4–23, and young are 8–12 inches (20–30 cm) long.

Similar Species   The red diamond rattlesnake (34) is pink to reddish-brown, lacks the conspicuous black dots in its body blotches, and the first pair of lower labials is usually divided transversely. The Mojave rattlesnake (38) has enlarged scales between the supraoculars, narrow black tail rings, and a white stripe behind the eye which extends back behind the corner of the mouth. The speckled rattlesnake (35) usually has salt-and-pepper markings. Also, the prenasals are usually separated from the rostral by small scales, or the supraoculars are pitted, deeply furrowed, or have broken outer edges.

Notes   This snake is responsible for more snakebite deaths than any other in the country, not only for the reasons listed above, but also because it is extensively hunted by amateurs for "rattlesnake round-ups" held throughout the Southwest. It is a very dangerous snake and should be left alone.

Subspecies   There are no subspecies of this snake.

Western Diamondback Rattlesnake

Crotalus atrox

At A Glance

- *Venomous*
- *Size:* 30 to 84 inches (76 to 213 cm)
- *Large & thick-bodied*

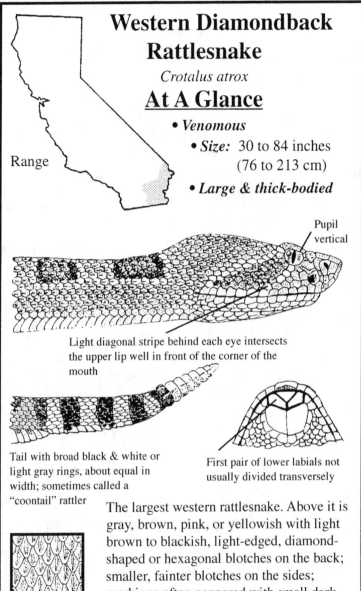

Range

Pupil vertical

Light diagonal stripe behind each eye intersects the upper lip well in front of the corner of the mouth

Tail with broad black & white or light gray rings, about equal in width; sometimes called a "coontail" rattler

First pair of lower labials not usually divided transversely

Scales keeled, in 25 to 27 rows

The largest western rattlesnake. Above it is gray, brown, pink, or yellowish with light brown to blackish, light-edged, diamond-shaped or hexagonal blotches on the back; smaller, fainter blotches on the sides; markings often peppered with small dark spots, giving the snake a "dusty" appearance overall. Young have more distinct markings than adults.

34 Red Diamond Rattlesnake

Cascabel Diamante Rojo

Crotalus exsul Garman 1883

krotalon, Greek = a little bell, a rattle; *exsulo*, Latin = to be an exile

This species name was originally given to the Cedros Island diamond rattlesnake, which was restricted ("exiled") to that island off the Pacific coast of Baja California. Mainland red diamond rattlesnakes have now been shown to be the same species (see notes).

Habitat   This snake inhabits desert scrub, open chaparral, grassland, woodland, mesquite and cactus environments along with rocky alluvial fans or canyons. It is found on both the coastal and desert sides of the mountains and occurs out onto the desert floor.

Prey   The red diamond rattlesnake eats rabbits, rodents, and birds.

Behavior   This large rattler is similar to its close relative, the Western diamondback rattlesnake. It is active at dusk and at night, particularly in hot weather, but it is also abroad in the daytime during cooler periods. It is generally less aggressive than the Western diamondback and less prone to hold its ground, but this may vary with the individual.

Reproduction   Like other rattlesnakes, the red diamond is a live-bearing snake. Three–20 young are born in the summer, and young range from 11.8–13.8 inches (30–35 cm) in length.

Similar Species   The Western diamondback rattlesnake (33) has distinctive black speckling in the blotches of its pattern, and the first lower labials are not usually divided transversely.

Notes   This snake has been known as *Crotalus ruber* Cope 1892 since its original description (*ruber*, Latin = red). However, recent studies by Grismer et al. (1994) and Murphy et al. (1995) have shown that it is nearly indistinguishable biochemically from *C. exsul* of Cedros Island in the Pacific Ocean off Baja California. They, therefore, confirm what others had suspected, that the two should be considered a single species. Since the name *C. exsul* had priority, that is, it was the older of the two names, it took precedence over the other, even though it had been in common use for so many years. The name change may be challenged by some who feel that the historical use of *ruber* should take precedence over the priority rule, but this remains to be seen. I am herein agreeing with Grismer et al. and Murphy et al.

Subspecies   One subspecies is found in California.

Red Diamond Rattlesnake

Crotalus exsul

At A Glance

- *Venomous*

- *Size:* 30 to 65 inches (75 to 162 cm)

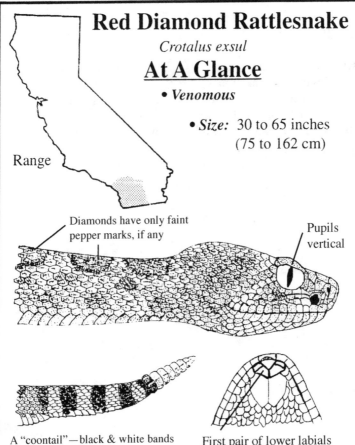

Range

Diamonds have only faint pepper marks, if any

Pupils vertical

A "coontail"—black & white bands of equal width contrast sharply with ground color of body

First pair of lower labials usually divided transversely

Scales keeled, in 29 rows

A tan, pink, rust-colored, reddish, or brick red snake; diamonds on the back are usually light-edged. The young are dark gray at first, but soon change to reddish-brown.

Northern Red Rattlesnake

Crotalus exsul ruber (Kallert, 1927) (Murphy et al., 1995)

Distinguishing Characteristics   This is the only subspecies of this snake that enters the United States—others occur in Mexico. This snake has brick red to pink-ish-tan diamonds, usually uniformly colored, with no light areas. The ground color is pinkish-gray to tan, and there is little or no pattern on the head.

35 Speckled Rattlesnake

Víbora Blanca

Crotalus mitchelli (Cope, 1861)

krotalon, Greek = a little bell, a rattle; mitchelli, honoring Dr. S. Weir Mitchell, who researched rattlesnake venom in the 1860s

Habitat   Over much of its range this snake is a rock-dweller, but it is also found in sandy areas and desert flats. It occurs in sagebrush and creosote bush flats, and chaparral, cactus, and piñon-juniper woodland areas.

Prey   This rattler eats small mammals (mice, kangaroo rats, ground squirrels, wood rats, etc.), lizards (spiny lizards, side-blotched lizards, whiptails, etc.), and birds.

Behavior   The speckled rattlesnake is active both in the daytime and at dusk and becomes nocturnal with hotter weather. It is usually an alert and nervous snake, quick to rattle and prone to hold its ground when annoyed.

Reproduction   Live bearing, with 2–11 young born from July to August. The young are 8–12 inches (20–30 cm) long at birth.

Similar Species   The Western diamondback rattlesnake (33) has "coontail" markings and does not have pitted and creased supraoculars or small scales between the prenasals and rostral. The Mojave rattlesnake (38) has enlarged scales between the supraoculars and usually a better defined dorsal pattern.

Notes   This snake is highly variable in color and pattern and sometimes the pattern, if any, is vague, while other times it may be distinct diamonds, hexagonal, or hourglass-shaped blotches.

Subspecies   Two subspecies of this snake are recognized in California.

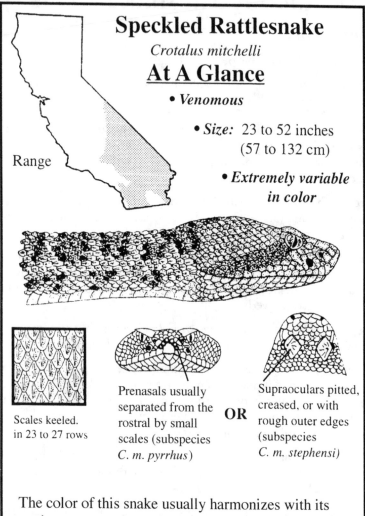

Speckled Rattlesnake
Crotalus mitchelli
At A Glance

- *Venomous*
- *Size:* 23 to 52 inches (57 to 132 cm)
- *Extremely variable in color*

Range

Scales keeled. in 23 to 27 rows

Prenasals usually separated from the rostral by small scales (subspecies *C. m. pyrrhus*)

OR

Supraoculars pitted, creased, or with rough outer edges (subspecies *C. m. stephensi)*

The color of this snake usually harmonizes with its environment, and may be tan, cream, gray, yellowish, pink, brown, or black. There are very dark specimens on Pisgah lava flow in the Mojave Desert. Some specimens with rough scales and peppered patterns resemble decomposed granite. Markings, sometimes vague, may be bands, hexagonal blotches, hourglass shapes, or diamonds. The tail has dark rings.

Southwestern Speckled Rattlesnake

Crotalus mitchelli pyrrhus (Cope, 1866)

pyrrhus, Latin = reddish, orange, or flame-colored

Distinguishing Characteristics   Small scales usually separate the rostral from the prenasals in this subspecies. The supraoculars are unmodified (not pitted or creased or with rough outer edges). The ground color is highly variable—white to gray or varying shades of pink or orange. The dark bands on the back are often split by a lighter color.

Panamint Rattlesnake

Crotalus mitchelli stephensi Klauber, 1930

stephensi, honoring Frank Stephens who was a member of the collecting team that brought in the first specimen of this subspecies

Distinguishing Characteristics   There are no small scales between the rostral and the prenasals. The supraoculars are often pitted, deeply creased, or appear to have irregular outer edges. The color is usually tan or gray, with light brown blotches or bands, which are more regular in outline and more distinctly edged in white than those of *C. m. pyrrhus.*

36 Sidewinder

Víbora Cornuda

Crotalus cerastes Hallowell, 1854

krotalon, Greek = a little bell, a rattle; *cerastes,* Latin = a horned serpent

Habitat   The sidewinder is a species of the deserts, most often found in areas of loose, wind-blown sand, but also in hardpan flats and rocky areas. It is common around hummocks topped by creosote or other bushes that provide burrowing areas for kangaroo rats and other rodents.

Prey   Sidewinders eat pocket mice, kangaroo rats, lizards, and occasionally birds. Young sidewinders prefer small lizards, while older and larger snakes favor rodents. Rodents are bitten, released, and tracked down, but lizards are generally held until the venom takes effect (Secor, 1994).

Behavior   Sidewinders are active at a greater range of temperatures than many other snakes, having been recorded out and about at temperatures from 64–99°F (17.5–37°C). They are most active at night, but also in the mornings and at dusk. In daytime, they will often "crater" into the sand at the base of a bush or seek shelter under flat boards. If the weather becomes too hot or too cold, they will retreat into an animal burrow. The sidewinding form of locomotion, in which they throw their bodies in sideways, S-shaped loops with only two parts of the body touching the ground at any time, is particularly effective in loose dune sand and is distinctive of this species.

Reproduction   Sidewinder young are born alive, spring through fall. Anywhere from 4–18 young are born at lengths of 6.5–8 inches (17–20 cm).

Similar Species   The upturned, pointed supraoculars distinguish this snake from any other California snake.

Notes   The "horns" of the sidewinder appear to act as sunshades, reducing the sun's glare in the snake's eyes, and probably allowing it to more accurately ambush its lizard prey in the daytime (Stebbins, 1985).

Subspecies   Two subspecies of the sidewinder are found in California.

Sidewinder

Crotalus cerastes

At A Glance

- *Venomous*

  - *Size:* 17 to 33 inches (42 to 82 cm)

    - *The "horned" rattlesnake*

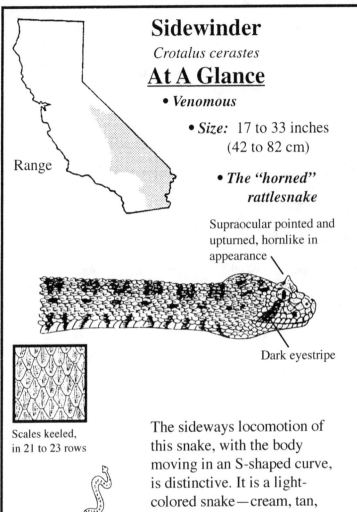

Range

Supraocular pointed and upturned, hornlike in appearance

Dark eyestripe

Scales keeled, in 21 to 23 rows

The sideways locomotion of this snake, with the body moving in an S-shaped curve, is distinctive. It is a light-colored snake—cream, tan, pink, or gray—usually harmonizing with its environment; patterned with darker blotches on the back, which may be grayish, yellowish-brown, or tan.

Mojave Desert Sidewinder

Crotalus cerastes cerastes Hallowell, 1854

Distinguishing Characteristics   The basal segment of the rattle is brown in adults. There are usually 21 scale rows at midbody.

Colorado Desert Sidewinder

Crotalus cerastes laterorepens Klauber, 1944

lateris, Latin = the side, or flank; *repens,* Latin = creeping, crawling (literally, "crawling sideways")

Distinguishing Characteristics   The basal segment of the rattle in adults is black. There are usually 23 dorsal scale rows at midbody.

37 Western Rattlesnake

Cascabel Occidental

Crotalus viridis (Rafinesque, 1818*)*

krotalon, Greek = a little bell, a rattle; *viridis,* Latin = various shades of green

Habitat   This snake, which has a huge range throughout the West, is the most widely distributed venomous snake in North America. It inhabits a wide array of habitats. In California, it can be found in coastal sage scrub, chaparral, grassland and oak woodland areas, along with conifer forests and hillsides down to the desert's edge. Rocky outcrops, rocky hillsides, talus slopes, stream courses, and areas with lots of down logs are favorite haunts for this snake. It is found from sea level to 10,000 feet in elevation.

Prey   The Western rattlesnake eats rodents (mice, rats, ground squirrels, gophers, etc.) and other small mammals (rabbits, moles, shrews), birds and their eggs and nestlings, lizards, snakes, and amphibians.

Behavior   This species is generally active at dusk and during daylight, but will become nocturnal in very hot weather. In cold weather, particularly in the northern parts of the state or at high elevations, it may den up in rock crevices, caves, or animal burrows, sometimes in great numbers. They are active at temperatures ranging from 68–95°F (20–35°C).

Reproduction   Mating occurs often in the late summer or fall, but spring mating is also possible. Sperm are stored over the winter and ovulation and fertilization occur the following spring. One–25 young are born alive in late summer or early fall, at lengths of 7–12 inches (17.8–30.5 cm).

Similar Species   The Western rattlesnake is the only species with more than two internasals in contact with the rostral scale.

Notes   This species, in particular *C. v. helleri* (see below), also occurs on Santa Catalina Island off the coast from Los Angeles. It is this subspecies, too, that is said to hybridize with the Mojave rattlesnake (48) in the western Antelope Valley, Los Angeles County (Stebbins, 1985).

Subspecies   Three subspecies of this rattlesnake are found within California's borders.

VIPERS AND PIT VIPERS

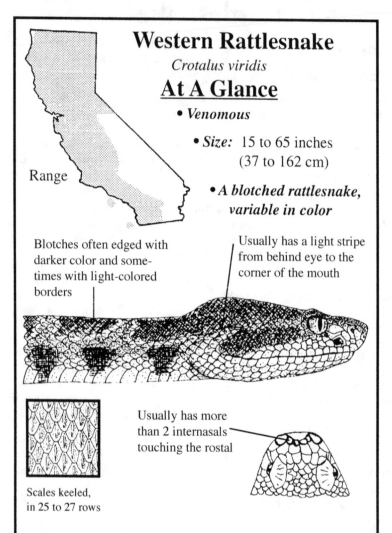

Western Rattlesnake

Crotalus viridis

At A Glance

- *Venomous*

  - *Size:* 15 to 65 inches
    (37 to 162 cm)

    - *A blotched rattlesnake,
      variable in color*

Range

Blotches often edged with
darker color and some-
times with light-colored
borders

Usually has a light stripe
from behind eye to the
corner of the mouth

Usually has more
than 2 internasals
touching the rostal

Scales keeled,
in 25 to 27 rows

This snake varies widely in color over its extensive
range; often its ground color harmonizes with the soil
color it is found on. It may be cream, yellowish, gray,
greenish, pink, brown, or black. Blotches usually give
way to crossbands toward the tail. The tail has light
and dark rings, but they do not usually contrast
sharply with the body color.

Southern Pacific Rattlesnake

Crotalus viridis helleri Meek, 1905

Distinguishing Characteristics   This snake is usually dark in coloration: gray, olive, tan, or black above with darker large blotches. The blotches are angular and light-edged. A single loreal scale is present. The terminal dark tail ring is poorly defined and about twice as wide as the others.

Great Basin Rattlesnake

Crotalus viridis lutosus Klauber, 1930

lutosus, Latin = muddy, of a clay-yellow color

Distinguishing Characteristics   This subspecies is usually buff, pale yellow, light gray, or tan in color, with contrasting brown to blackish blotches that are about as wide as the spaces between them.

Northern Pacific Rattlesnake

Crotalus viridis oreganus Holbrook, 1840

oreganus, Latin = belonging to Oregon

Distinguishing Characteristics   The dark tail rings of this subspecies are well defined and of quite uniform width. Young of this subspecies have bright yellow tails. Color and patterns are variable throughout its range.

38 Mojave Rattlesnake

Chiauhcoatl

Crotalus scutulatus (Kennicott, 1861)

krotalon, Greek = a little bell, a rattle; *scutulatus*, Latin = diamond- or lozenge-shaped (a reference to the dorsal pattern)

Habitat   This rattlesnake primarily inhabits upland desert and lower mountain slopes, but ranges down to sea level near the mouth of the Colorado River. Habitats vary from creosote bush flats to rocky canyons and grassland, open juniper woodland, and light chaparral areas. Despite its name, it is found in the Colorado (Sono-

Figure 5. Mojave rattlesnake

ran) Desert as well as the Mojave and extends eastward to the Chihuahuan Desert.

Prey   The Mojave rattler eats kangaroo rats and other rodents, and probably other reptiles such as lizards. One was observed attempting to swallow a desert horned lizard at the Desert Tortoise Natural Area in the Mojave Desert (Bryan Jennings, 1992).

Behavior   The Mojave rattlesnake is active in both the daytime and at dusk during cool weather, and during hot periods it becomes nocturnal. It is a very alert, excitable, and aggressive snake, and possesses a very potent venom with a higher proportion of neurotoxic properties than most rattlesnake venoms.

Reproduction   The Mojave rattlesnake has 2–13 (average 8) young, born live in July or August. Newborn snakes are 8.6–11.1 inches (22–28.3 cm) long.

Similar Species   The Western diamondback rattlesnake (33) has a less well-defined dorsal pattern with conspicuous black speckling in it. It has no enlarged scales on the snout or between the supraoculars. The Western rattlesnake (37) has more than four internasals in contact with the rostral scale. The speckled rattlesnake (35) has prenasals separated from the rostral by small scales; or, the supraoculars are pitted, deeply furrowed, or have irregular outer edges.

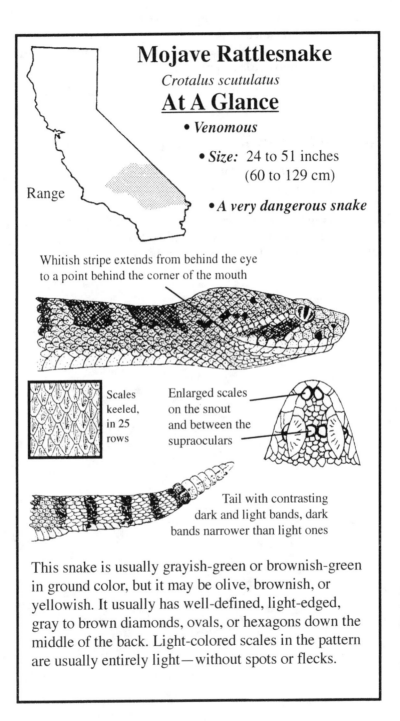

Mojave Rattlesnake

Crotalus scutulatus

At A Glance

- *Venomous*

  - *Size:* 24 to 51 inches (60 to 129 cm)

  - *A very dangerous snake*

Range

Whitish stripe extends from behind the eye to a point behind the corner of the mouth

Scales keeled, in 25 rows

Enlarged scales on the snout and between the supraoculars

Tail with contrasting dark and light bands, dark bands narrower than light ones

This snake is usually grayish-green or brownish-green in ground color, but it may be olive, brownish, or yellowish. It usually has well-defined, light-edged, gray to brown diamonds, ovals, or hexagons down the middle of the back. Light-colored scales in the pattern are usually entirely light—without spots or flecks.

VIPERS AND PIT VIPERS

Notes   This is an extremely dangerous snake due to its irascibility and its potent, diversified venom. A leading authority on snakebites and venoms, Dr. Frederick Shannon, was killed by the bite of this snake while attempting to capture one.

Subspecies   One subspecies of the Mojave rattlesnake is found in California.

Mojave Green Rattlesnake

Crotalus scutulatus scutulatus
(Kennicott, 1961)

Distinguishing Characteristics   This is the only sub-species of this snake that enters the United States. Its characteristics are listed in the At A Glance table.

The Snake That Never Was, and Other Loose Ends

Just as there are subspecies that are in question, some distribution records are also in dispute. I ran across two of them while researching this book. I began my study by looking at three state checklists (Griffith, 1966; Jennings, 1983, 1987). After compiling the lists, I used them as a base to determine which species to research further and which subspecies to determine valid.

Jennings (1987) listed the regal ringneck snake, *Diadophis punctatus regalis,* as occurring in California. This sent me on a search of the literature, but I was able to find only one other source (Behler and King, 1979) that listed it as ranging to southeastern California. None of the books with range maps showed it occurring here, and the closest I could determine from any of the sources I used was in Yavapai and Pima counties, Arizona (Fowlie, 1965). While I am not claiming that my search was exhaustive, I did not come to the conclusion that this subspecies is currently recognized within California, and I have not included it in this book.

In looking through one of those sources (Wright and Wright, 1957), I did come across a range map that showed the banded sand snake, *Chilomeniscus cinctus*, occurring in southeastern California. This species had not shown up on any of the checklists. Schmidt and Davis (1953) also stated that it had been found in California, but Stebbins (1954, 1966, 1985) did not show the banded sand snake as reaching into the state (although they appear to come very close to the southeast corner where Baja California and Arizona are adjacent). I then proceeded to e-mail various sources around the state to determine whether any of the major collections had any specimens of *Chilomeniscus* or any records of them from California. In a very gratifying response, I heard from all my sources, some of whom referred me to others. In this way I was able to track down the source of the reports that said this species is in California.

The story begins in 1861 with Edward Drinker Cope, colorful naturalist at the Academy of Natural Sciences in Philadelphia. In that year he described a new species of *Chilomeniscus*, collected and submitted by a Dr. George H. Horn from Owens Valley, California. Cope described it as *Chilomeniscus ephippicus*. In 1917, Grinnell and Camp, listed two specimens of *C. ephippicus* that were collected in California: "A mutilated specimen was found by us near Fort Yuma, California." The other was listed as being from the type locality (Owens Valley, Inyo County). By the time John Van Denburgh produced his book *The Reptiles of Western North America*, 1922, *C. ephippicus* had become *C. cinctus*, in his view. Schmidt and Davis (1953) and Wright and Wright (1957) were probably citing these records when they included this distribution in their books.

Banta and Leviton (1963) did an exhaustive study on the genus *Chilomeniscus*. They came to the conclusion that the citing of Owens Valley as the site of collection was "probably in error. No specimens of Chilomeniscus have since been reported from California, although many areas in southern California, which could provide suitable habitats for this animal, have been more intensely searched than most any other comparable area in the world. Based on our study we are unable to come to a definite conclusion as to the exact source of the type material of this form. Though we think it probably came from northern Baja California, we are not sure. We are certain, however, that it was not taken in California's Owens Valley."

The banded sand snake is a small (around 7–10 inches) snake, even more highly adapted to burrowing than the Western shovelnose snake (27). Its head is no wider than its neck, the lower jaw is deeply inset, the snout is flat, nasal valves are present, the eyes are small and turned upward, and the belly is angular on each side. It lives in sand or loamy soil, through which it "swims" efficiently and seldom emerges on the surface except at night. It eats centipedes, sand-burrowing cockroaches, and probably ant pupae and other insects. It is variable in color and pattern, being whitish, pale yellow, or reddish-orange with anywhere from 19–49 black or dark-brown crossbands on the dorsum.

Since there are no California specimens in the major collections, and Klauber and other eminent scientists and collectors have not found it here, I have not included it in this book. Although a couple of the people I communicated with feel that it could still turn up in the Algodones Dunes or the Winterhaven area, it apparently hasn't yet done so.

Figure 6. Banded sand snake

Other individual snakes are occasionally listed as having been found in California, almost always in residential areas. These include the emerald tree boa, *Corallus caninus*; tree boa, *C. enydris*; boa constrictor, *Boa constrictor*; Burmese python, *Python molurus bivittatus*; reticulated python, *Python reticulatus*; corn snake, *Elaphe guttata guttata*; Eastern indigo snake, *drymarchon corais couperi*; Florida kingsnake, *Lampropeltis getula floridana*; banded water snake, *Nerodia fasciata fasciata*; Northern water snake, *N. sipedon sipedon*; cat-eyed snake, *Leptodeira annulata*; Eastern ribbon snake, *Thamnophis sauritus*; rough green snake, *Opheodrys aestivus*; and even one Egyptian cobra, *Naja haje* (Jennings, 1987)! I'm personally aware of a Sinaloan milk snake, *Lampropeltis triangulum sinaloae*; African house snake, *Lamprophis fuliginosus*; Great Plains rat snake, *Elaphe guttata emoryi*; and banded water snake, *Nerodia fasciata* found loose in my own neighborhood. Tree boas and cat-eyed snakes apparently were common in banana shipments to southern California before such cargo was routinely gassed on entry into the United States. Others are all probably escaped or intentionally released pets or captives (including the cobra). This is a situation that will undoubtedly become worse as the reptile pet trade continues to expand, and it is particularly a problem in cities, where the majority of pet shops and their patrons live. Many of these exotics are unable to survive the winter outdoors. None of the imported snakes have been found to be breeding or forming wild populations in California.

Conservation and The Law

In California, native amphibians and reptiles are covered by regulations in the Fish and Game Code. Over the years, these regulations have changed from benign neglect of most species to today's rules, which attempt to protect those species in decline while regulating the "take" on others so that the resource is used wisely. While some of these regulations apply to snakes only, few do so without connection to other creatures. This chapter presents Title 14 of the California Fish and Game Code. *These regulations change frequently, so obtain the most recent regulations before any field excursions.*

The definitions that follow (taken directly from Title 14 of the California Code of Regulations, with the appropriate sections cited in parentheses) will help in understanding the regulations.

Native Reptiles and Amphibians: Native reptiles and amphibians are those subspecies, and species which have no subspecies in California, including all color phases, of the classes Reptilia and Amphibia indigenous to California whether taken from the wild or produced in captivity. (T14 1.67)

Bag and Possession Limit: No more than one daily bag limit of each kind of fish, amphibian, reptile, mollusk or crustacean named in these regulations may be taken or possessed by any one person unless otherwise authorized; regardless of whether they are fresh, frozen, or otherwise preserved. (T14 1.17)

Take: Hunt, pursue, catch, capture or kill fish, amphibians, reptiles, mollusks, crustaceans or invertebrates or attempting to do so. (T14 1.80)

The materials reprinted here are the latest available at the time of printing; they became effective in September 1996. It is always a good idea to check for the latest regulations, as they have been changed slightly every two years or so for the past two decades. Sporting goods stores or fishing supply shops usually have free copies of the fishing regulations available. Also, you may note some discrepancies in the way common and scientific names appear herein as opposed to the rest of the book. I have left them the way they appear in the Fish and Game materials. As mentioned elsewhere in this book, few authorities agree 100 percent on usage of names, and it is still obvious which creatures are being considered here.

One last note—in order to collect or possess native reptiles and amphibians in the state of California, anyone 16 years or older must have a valid sportfishing license!

"Anyone 16 years and older must have a fishing license to take any kind of fish, mollusk, invertebrate, amphibians or crustacean in California . . . A license is required to take reptiles, except for rattlesnakes . . . Only a basic fishing license is required to take amphibians, reptiles (except rattlesnakes) . . . Every person while engaged in taking any fish, amphibian, or reptile shall display their valid sport fishing license by attaching it to outer clothing at or above the waistline so that it is plainly visible . . . The law now provides for a fine of not less than $250 for fishing without a license." (T14 700)

T14 40. General Provisions Relating to Native Reptiles and Amphibians

(a) Prohibition on Take, Possession, Purchase, Propagation, Sale, Import, or Export. It is unlawful to take, possess, purchase, propagate, sell, transport, import, or export any native reptile or amphibian, or part thereof, except as provided in this chapter and in Chapter 2 of this subdivision relating to sportfishing and frogging.

(b) Except for dried or processed reptile skins, it is unlawful to display, in any place of business where pets or other animals are sold, native reptiles or amphibians which cannot be lawfully sold.

(c) Progeny resulting from pregnant native reptiles or amphibians collected from the wild must be transferred to another person or to a scientific or educational institution within 45 days of birth or hatching. Persons receiving such progeny shall comply with the bag and possession limits specified in sections 41.5 and 42.5.

(d) Reptiles or amphibians which have been in captivity, including wild-caught and captively-bred individuals or offspring, shall not be released into the wild.

(e) Biological Supply Houses and Exempt Organizations.

(1) Biological Supply Houses. The department may issue permits to owners of biological supply houses to sell native reptiles and amphibians to scientific or educational institutions, pursuant to Section 651 of these regulations

(2) Organizations and Schools Exempt from Permit. Institutions or organizations engaged in bona fide scientific study of native wildlife, whose specimens are readily available for use or viewing by the public at large on a regular basis, and government accredited schools that are open to the public may possess, accept donations of, or exchange, purchase or sell between organizations, native reptiles and amphibians without a permit.

(f) Except as otherwise provided in federal law, the Fish and Game Code or Section 671, no permit is required to import, export, transport, possess, propagate, buy or sell nonnative reptiles or amphibians.

T14 41. Protected Amphibians

Except under special permit from the department issued pursuant to sections 650 and 670.7 of these regulations, or Section 2081 of the Fish and Game Code, none of the following amphibians may be taken or possessed at any time:

(a) Santa Cruz long-toed salamander (*Ambystoma macrodactylum croceum*)

(b) Siskyou mountain salamander (*Plethodon stormi*)

(c) Desert slender salamander (*Batrachoseps aridus*)

(d) Kern Canyon slender salamander (*Batrachoseps simatus*)

(e) Tehachapi slender salamander (*Batrachoseps stebbinsi*)

(f) Limestone salamander (*Hydromantes brunus*)

(g) Shasta salamander (*Hydromantes shastae*)

(h) Black toad (*Bufo exsul*)

(i) Red-legged frog (*Rana aurora*)

(j) Southwestern toad (*Bufo microscaphus*)

(k) Mt. Lyell salamander (*Hydromantes platycephalus*)

(l) Inyo Mountains salamander (*Batrachoseps campi*)

(m) California tiger salamander (*Ambystoma californiense*)

(n) Olympic salamander (*Rhyacotriton olympicus*)

(o) Del Norte salamander (*Plethodon elongatus*)

(p) Colorado River toad (*Bufo alvarius*)

(q) Yosemite toad (*Bufo canorus*)

(r) Foothill yellow-legged frog (*Rana boylii*)

(s) Mountain yellow-legged frog (*Rana muscosa*)

(t) Cascade frog (*Rana cascadae*)

(u) Spotted frog (*Rana pretiosa*)

(v) Lowland leopard frog (*Rana yavapaiensis*)

(w) Tailed frog (*Ascaphus truei*)

(x) Western spadefoot (*Scaphiopus hammondii*)

T14 41.5. Amphibians Except Protected Amphibians

Native amphibians may be taken under the authority of a sportfishing license under the following conditions:

(a) Open season: All year.

(b) Limit: The bag and possession limit on native amphibians species, in the aggregate of all subspecies, not listed in section 41 is four, except as provided in Section 43.

(c) Hours: Amphibians may be taken at any time of day or night.

(d) Methods of take: Amphibians may be taken only by hand, hand-held dip net or hook and line, except bullfrogs may be taken as authorized in Section 5.05.

(e) Special closures:

(1) No amphibians may be taken from ecological reserves designated by the commission in Section 630 or from state parks, or national parks or monuments.

(2) No slender salamanders (*Batrachoseps* ssp.) may be taken from the Santa Rosa Mountains, Riverside County.

(3) No salamanders of the genera *Batrachoseps* or *Hydromantes* may be taken in Inyo and Mono counties.

T14 42. Protected Reptiles

Except under special permit from the department issued pursuant to sections 650 and 670.5 of these regulations, or section 2081 of the

Fish and Game Code, none of the following reptiles may be taken or possessed at any time:

(a) Blunt-nosed leopard lizard (*Gambelia sila*)
(b) Banded Gila monster (*Heloderma suspectum cinctum*)
(c) Southern rubber boa (*Charina bottae umbratica*)
(d) Alameda whipsnake (*Masticophis lateralis euryxanthus*)
(e) San Francisco garter snake (*Thamnophis sirtalis tetrataenia*)
(f) Giant garter snake (*Thamnophis gigas*)
(g) Desert tortoise (*Gopherus agassizi*)
(h) Panamint alligator lizard (*Gerrhonotus panamintinus*)
(i) Sonora mud turtle (*Kinosternon sonoriense*)
(j) Island night lizard (*Xantusia riversiana*)
(k) Flat-tailed horned lizard (*Phrynosoma mcallii*)
(l) San Diego mountain kingsnake (*Lampropeltis zonata pulchra*)
(m) Coachella Valley fringe-toed lizard (*Uma inornata*)
(n) Switak's barefoot gecko (*Coleonyx switaki*)
(o) Leaf-toed gecko (*Phyllodactylus xanti*)
(p) Granite night lizard (*Xantusia henshawi*)
(q) Orange-throated whiptail (*Cnemidophorus hyperythrus*)
(r) Black legless lizard (*Anniella pulchra nigra*)
(s) Coast horned lizard (*Phrynosoma coronatum*)
(t) Western pond turtle (*Clemmys marmorata*)
(u) San Joaquin Coachwhip (*Masticophis flagellum ruddocki*)
(v) Two-striped garter snake (*Thamnophis hammondii*)

T14 42.5. Reptiles Except Protected Reptiles

Native reptiles may be taken under the authority of a sportfishing license under the following conditions:

(a) Open season: All year.
(b) Limit: The bag and possession limit on all native reptile species, in the aggregate of all subspecies, not listed in Section 42 is two, except as provided in Section 43 and as follows:
  (1) Spiny softshell turtle (*Trionyx spiniferus* ssp.): Five
  (2) California legless lizard (*Anniella pulchra* ssp.): One
  (3) California mountain kingsnake (*Lampropeltis zonata* ssp.): One
  (4) Western fence lizard (*Sceloporus occidentalis* ssp.), sagebrush lizard (*Sceloporus graciosus* ssp.), side-blotched lizard (*Uta stansburiana* ssp.), desert night lizard (*Xantusia vigilis* ssp.), and western skink (*Eumeces skiltonianus* ssp.): 25 in the aggregate

(5) California subspecies of gopher snakes (*Pituophis melanoleucus* ssp.) and California common kingsnake (*Lampropeltis getulus californiae*): Four

(c) Hours: Reptiles may be taken at any time of day or night.

(d) Methods of take:

    (1) Reptiles may not be injured and may be taken only by hand, except as provided in subsections (C), (2) and (3) below, or by the following hand-operated devices:

        (A) Lizard nooses

        (B) Snake tongs

        (C) Snake hooks

    (2) Rattlesnakes may be taken by any method.

    (3) Turtles may be taken by hook and line.

    (4) It is unlawful to use any method or means of collecting that involves breaking apart of rocks, granite flakes, logs or other shelters in or under which reptiles may be found.

(e) Special Closures:

    (1) No reptiles may be taken from ecological reserves designated by the commission in Section 630 or from state parks, or national parks or monuments.

    (2) No California mountain kingsnakes may be taken in San Diego and Orange counties or in Los Angeles County west of Interstate 5.

    (3) No common garter snakes (*Thamnophis sirtalis* ssp.) may be taken in Ventura, Los Angeles, Orange, Riverside and San Diego counties.

Other regulations that are outside the scope of this book include the captive propagation and commercialization of native reptiles and amphibians, collecting permits, importation, transportation and possession of wild animals, and others. People interested in these rules are encouraged to contact the California Department of Fish and Game.

In addition to being protected by the general regulations above, a few reptiles and amphibians also have extra protectional status by being considered threatened or endangered species by the state.

T14 670.5 Animals of California Declared to be Endangered or Threatened

The following species and subspecies are hereby declared to be endangered or threatened:

(a) Endangered
   (3) Amphibians
      (A) Santa Cruz long-toed salamander (*Ambystoma macro-dactylum croceum*)
      (B) Desert slender salamander (*Batrachoseps aridus*)
      (C) Southwestern toad (*Bufo microscaphus*)
   (4) Reptiles
      (A) Coachella Valley fringe-toed lizard (*Uma inornata*)
      (B) Blunt-nosed leopard lizard (*Gambelia sila*)
      (C) San Francisco garter snake (*Thamnophis sirtalis tetrataenia*)
(b) Threatened
   (3) Amphibians
      (A) Siskyou mountain salamander (*Plethodon stormi*)
      (B) Kern Canyon slender salamander (*Batrachoseps simatus*)
      (C) Tehachapi slender salamander (*Batrachoseps stebbinsi*)
      (D) Limestone salamander (*Hydromantes brunus*)
      (E) Shasta salamander (*Hydromantes shastae*)
      (F) Black toad (*Bufo exsul*)
      (G) Red-legged frog (*Rana aurora*)
   (4) Reptiles:
      (A) Desert tortoise (*Gopherus agassizi*)
      (B) Barefoot banded gecko (*Coleonyx switaki*)
      (C) Southern rubber boa (*Charina bottae umbratica*)
      (D) Alameda whipsnake (*Masticophis lateralis euryxanthus*)
      (E) Giant garter snake (*Thamnophis couchi gigas*)

The following have the added protection of federal law under the Endangered Species Act:

Threatened

Red-legged frog (*Rana aurora*)
Arroyo Southwestern toad (*Bufo microscaphus californicus*)
Desert tortoise (*Gopherus agassizi*)
Coachella Valley fringe-toed lizard (*Uma inornata*)
Island night lizard (*Xantusia riversiana*)
Giant garter snake (*Thamnophis gigas*)

Endangered

Santa Cruz long-toed salamander (*Ambystoma macrodactylum croceum*)
Desert slender salamander (*Batrachoseps aridus*)
Blunt-nosed leopard lizard (*Gambelia sila*)

San Francisco garter snake (*Thamnophis sirtalis tetrataenia*)

Laws and regulations aside, snakes and their relatives need our help. With 40 million people residing in California, the pressures upon wild populations of wildlife are intense. For snakes it is worse than for other creatures—there are few animals a person will needlessly kill as readily as a serpent. As the numbers of people that come into contact with snakes increase, this problem likewise increases. This does not even take into account road kills, both deliberate and accidental, that annihilate untold numbers of reptiles annually.

The biggest problem facing reptiles in California is habitat destruction. Drainage of marshes and wetlands, plowing of open grasslands, channelization of creeks and building of dams on rivers, the building of highways, shopping malls, housing tracts, and industrial parks all deprive animals of habitat. Air, water, and soil are contaminated. Even formerly unacceptable areas for development, such as deserts and mountain slopes, are now being covered by urban and suburban development.

The awareness of this plight is not new. People have been working for decades to set aside parcels of land for the protection of wild resources. California boasts many fine state parks, including Anza-Borrego Desert State Park, the largest state park in the country. The Nature Conservancy and other "conservancy" groups have purchased tracts of land for the sole purpose of providing homes for wildlife and native vegetation. But saving isolated plots of land is not enough.

Anything living on an island has limitations to its population growth and movement—the edges of the island! For this reason, islands are immensely susceptible to environmental catastrophes. The introduction of the brown tree snake to the island of Guam is a classic example. The birds and small mammals of Guam had evolved outside the presence of a predator of this type and were wholly at its mercy—and it had none. Only taking some of the avian species into captivity saved them from total annihilation.

Building cities right up to the edges of preserves, surrounding them, in effect makes them islands. Aside from rats, cats, dogs, and humans that will inevitably invade these areas to the detriment of native species, many will be cut off from others of their kind. Many animals are genetically fragile—if their gene pool is limited, they will quickly decline.

So we need "wildlife corridors" between our reserves. But we need more than that. We need a whole new attitude about our place in the natural world. We need to allow more of nature to seep into our yards and cities, and we need to leave some areas inviolate. And, while we are developing this concept, we need to do all we can on an individual basis to preserve the reptiles with which we share our space. We need to observe them and learn about their life histories and environmental needs. We need to educate other people about the beauty and wonder of these creatures so that our children and theirs can still see snakes in a future California.

When researching this book, I used other books that are 50, 60 or more years old. The names are outdated in these old tomes, but the information is still good. It is my hope that this book will still be useful in 50 years, outdated though the names may be, to somebody trying to identify that sparkling streak of color they saw in a wild place in the wondrous state of California.

Herpetological Societies

In addition to those you may encounter in the wild, California reptiles may also be seen in zoos, museums, nature centers, and some city and county parks. These are good sources of information on these animals. More detailed information can be obtained from herpetological societies. These are generally groups of people interested in reptiles and amphibians who have banded together to share their mutual interest. Activities often include meetings with guest speakers, field trips, exhibitions, swap meets, conferences and symposia, and newsletters and other publications.

The following include some of California's herpetological societies:

American Federation of Herpetoculturists (AFH)
P. O. Box 300067
Escondido, CA 92030-0067

Asiac Herpetological Research Society
Museum of Vertebrate Zoology
University of California
Berkeley, CA 94720

Bay Area Amphibian and Reptile Society (BAARS)
c/o Palo Alto Junior Museum
1451 Middlefield Road
Palo Alto, CA 94301

Inland Empire Herpetological Society
San Bernardino County Museum
2024 Orange Tree Lane
Redlands, CA 92373

Kern County Herpetological Society
P. O. Box 762
Lebec, CA 93243-0762

North Bay Herpetological Society
c/o Melissa Kaplan
6366 Commerce Blvd. #216
Rohnert Park, CA 94928

Northern California Herpetological Society (NCHS)
P. O. Box 1363
Davis, CA 95617

San Diego Herpetological Society
P. O. Box 4036
San Diego, CA 92164

San Joaquin Herpetological Society
P. O. Box 634
Nevada City, CA 95959

Shasta Snake Society
P. O. Box 171
Douglas City, CA 96024

Southern California Herpetological Association
P. O. Box 2932
Santa Fe Springs, CA 90670

Southwestern Herpetologists Society
P. O. Box 7469
Van Nuys, CA 91409

Southwestern Herpetologists Society, Tri-Counties Chapter
P. O. Box 3881
Santa Barbara, CA 93130

APPENDIX B

Checklist of California Snakes

1. Leptotyphlops humilis	Western blind snake
Leptotyphlops humilis humilis	Southwestern blind snake
Leptotyphlops humilis cahuilae	Desert blind snake

2. Charina bottae	Rubber boa
Charina bottae bottae	Pacific rubber boa
Charina bottae umbratica	Southern rubber boa
Charina bottae utahensis	Rocky Mountain rubber boa

3. Lichanura trivirgata	Rosy boa
Lichanura trivirgata gracia	Desert rosy boa
Lichanura trivirgata roseofusca	Coastal rosy boa

4. Diadophis punctatus — Ringneck snake

Diadophis punctatus amabilis	Pacific ringneck snake
Diadophis punctatus modestus	San Bernardino ringneck snake
Diadophis punctatus occidentalis	Northwestern ringneck snake
Diadophis punctatus pulchellus	Coralbelly ringneck snake
Diadophis punctatus similis	San Diego ringneck snake
Diadophis punctatus vandenburghi	Monterey ringneck snake

5. Contia tenuis — Sharptail snake

6. Phyllorhynchus decurtatus — Spotted leafnose snake

Phyllorhynchus decurtatus perkinsi	Western leafnose snake

7. Coluber constrictor — Racer

Coluber constrictor mormon	Western yellowbelly racer

8. Masticophis flagellum — Coachwhip

Masticophis flagellum fuliginosus	Baja California coachwhip
Masticophis flagellum piceus	Red coachwhip (Red racer)
Masticophis flagellum ruddocki	San Joaquin coachwhip

9. Masticophis lateralis — Striped racer

Masticophis lateralis euryxanthus	Alameda striped racer
Masticophis lateralis lateralis	California striped racer

10. Masticophis taeniatus — Striped whipsnake

Masticophis taeniatus taeniatus	Desert striped whipsnake

11. Salvadora hexalepis — Western patchnose snake

Salvadora hexalepis hexalepis	Desert patchnose snake
Salvadora hexalepis mojavensis	Mojave patchnose snake
Salvadora hexalepis virgultea	Coast patchnose snake

12. Bogertophis rosaliae — Baja California rat snake

13. Arizona elegans — Glossy snake

Arizona elegans candida	Mojave glossy snake
Arizona elegans eburnata	Desert glossy snake
Arizona elegans occidentalis	California glossy snake

14. Pituophis catenifer — Gopher snake

Pituophis catenifer affinis	Sonoran gopher snake
Pituophis catenifer annectens	San Diego gopher snake
Pituophis catenifer catenifer	Pacific gopher snake
Pituophis catenifer deserticola	Great Basin gopher snake
Pituophis catenifer pumilis	Santa Cruz gopher snake

15. Lampropeltis getula — Common kingsnake

Lampropeltis getula californiae	California kingsnake

16. Lampropeltis zonata — California mountain kingsnake

Lampropeltis zonata multicincta	Sierra mountain kingsnake
Lampropeltis zonata multifasciata	Coast mountain kingsnake
Lampropeltis zonata parvirubra	San Bernardino mountain kingsnake
Lampropeltis zonata pulchra	San Diego mountain kingsnake
Lampropeltis zonata zonata	St. Helena mountain kingsnake

17. Rhinocheilus lecontei — Longnose snake

Rhinocheilus lecontei lecontei	Western longnose snake

18. Thamnophis sirtalis — Common garter snake

Thamnophis sirtalis fitchi	Valley garter snake
Thamnophis sirtalis infernalis	California red-sided garter snake
Thamnophis sirtalis tetrataenia	San Francisco garter snake

19. Thamnophis elegans — Western terrestrial garter snake

Thamnophis elegans elegans	Mountain garter snake
Thamnophis elegans biscutatus	Klamath garter snake
Thamnophis elegans terrestris	Coast garter snake
Thamnophis elegans vagrans	Wandering garter snake

20. Thamnophis atratus — Western aquatic garter snake

Thamnophis atratus atratus	Santa Cruz garter snake
Thamnophis atratus hydrophilus	Oregon garter snake

21. Thamnophis couchii — Sierra garter snake

22. Thamnophis gigas — Giant garter snake

23. Thamnophis hammondii — Two-striped garter snake

24. Thamnophis ordinoides	Northwestern garter snake
25. Thamnophis marcianus	Checkered garter snake
Thamnophis marcianus marcianus	Marcy's checkered garter snake
26. Sonora semiannulata	Ground snake
27. Chionactis occipitalis	Western shovelnose snake
Chionactis occipitalis occipitalis	Mojave shovelnose snake
Chionactis occipitalis annulata	Colorado Desert shovelnose snake
Chionactis occipitalis talpina	Nevada shovelnose snake
28. Tantilla planiceps	Western black-headed snake
29. Tantilla hobartsmithi	Southwestern black-headed snake
30. Trimorphodon biscutatus	Lyre snake
Trimorphodon biscutatus lambda	Sonoran lyre snake
Trimorphodon biscutatus vandenburghi	California lyre snake
31. Hypsiglena torquata	Night snake
Hypsiglena torquata deserticola	Desert night snake
Hypsiglena torquata klauberi	San Diego night snake
Hypsiglena torquata nuchalata	California night snake
32. Pelamis platurus	Yellowbelly sea snake
33. Crotalus atrox	Western diamondback rattlesnake
34. Crotalus exsul	Red diamond rattlesnake
Crotalus exsul ruber	Northern red rattlesnake
35. Crotalus mitchelli	Speckled rattlesnake
Crotalus mitchelli pyrrhus	Southwestern speckled rattlesnake
Crotalus mitchelli stephensi	Panamint rattlesnake
36. Crotalus cerastes	Sidewinder
Crotalus cerastes cerastes	Mojave Desert sidewinder
Crotalus cerastes laterorepens	Colorado Desert sidewinder

37. Crotalus viridis

Western rattlesnake

Crotalus viridis helleri	Southern Pacific rattlesnake
Crotalus viridis lutosus	Great Basin rattlesnake
Crotalus viridis oreganus	Northern Pacific rattlesnake

38. Crotalus scutulatus

Mojave rattlesnake

Crotalus scutulatus scutulatus	Mojave green rattlesnake

Glossary

Adaptation—A morphological, physiological, or behavioral feature that particularly suits an organism (or group of organisms) to its (their) way of life.

Adult—Fully grown (or nearly so) and sexually mature.

Advanced—Of more recent evolutionary origin.

Anal spur—A horny, pointed, sometimes hooked spur (a hind limb vestige), one on each side, just in front of the vent in boid snakes (boas and pythons).

Anterior—Before or toward the front.

Apical pits—Small paired pits or oval-shaped modifications near the free (apical) end of the scales of certain snakes.

Aquatic—Living in water.

Arboreal—Dwelling in trees or shrubs.

Arthropod—Animal usually with a hard, jointed external skeleton: crabs, insects, spiders, scorpions, etc.

Binomen—The name of a species consisting of the name of the genus in which it is classified followed by a word peculiar to the species; the equivalent of scientific name.

Brille—A transparent covering over the eye of a snake; also called the spectacle.

Caudal entire—An undivided caudal. In many snakes, the straplike scales that extend across the ventral surface of the tail are divided by a suture at the midline (referred to as pairs). Caudals are entire in rattlesnakes and most are entire in longnose snakes.

Cloaca—The common chamber into which the urinary, digestive, and reproductive systems discharge their contents, and which opens to the exterior.

Countersunk—Sunk beneath the margins of, as in the jaws of burrowing snakes, in which the lower jaw fits snugly within the margins of the upper jaw.

Crepuscular—Pertaining to activity at twilight.

Cycloid scales—Scales with free rear borders that are smoothly rounded.

Diurnal—Active by day.

Dorsal—Pertains to the upper surface (back) of the body.

Dorsolateral—Pertains to the upper sides of the body.

Dorsum—The upper, or dorsal, surface of the body including the tail.

Environment—All the factors, forces, or conditions that affect or influence the growth, development, and life of an organism.

Genus (plural: genera)—A category of classification ranking between the family and species; a group of structurally or phylogenetically related species or an isolated species exhibiting unusual differentiation (monotypic genus).

Gestation—Carrying or period of carrying the young, normally in the uterus, from conception to delivery.

Gravid—Laden with eggs; pregnant.

Habitat—The type of conditions in which an animal lives.

Hemipenis (plural: hemipenes)—One of the paired copulatory organs of snakes.

Hemorrhagic—Pertains to the loss of blood from the blood vessels. The hemorrhagic element in the venom of some snakes causes disintegration of blood cells and a breakdown of the vessel walls, resulting in a release of blood into the tissue spaces.

Hybrid—The offspring of the union of a male of one race, variety, species, genus, etc. with the female of another; a cross-bred animal.

Incubation—The act of incubating eggs, i.e., keeping them warm so that development is possible.

Intergrade—With reference to subspecies, to gradually merge one subspecies with another through a series of forms that are intermediate in color and/or structure.

Interspace—The patch of color between two markings (such as bands or blotches) on the back of a snake.

Keel—A lengthwise ridge on the scales of certain snakes.

Labium (plural: labia)—Lip.

Lateral stripe—A lengthwise stripe on the side of the body.

Maxillary bone—A bone on each side of the head forming most of the lateral border of the upper jaw and bearing most of the upper teeth.

Melanic—Dark; of the color of the pigment melanin, black or dark brown.

Melanism—The condition in which the melanic pigment is accentuated, sometimes to the point of obscuring all other color (such animals are called melanistic).

Monotypic—Having a single type or representative, as a genus with only one species.

Neurotoxin—A nerve poison.

Nocturnal—Active at night.

Ocular scale—In blind snakes, the scale overlying the vestigial eyes.

Oviparous—Producing eggs that hatch after laying.

Ovoviviparous—Producing eggs that have a well-developed shell or covering (as in oviparous animals), but which hatch within the body of the parent, as in the case of many snakes.

Ovum—A female germ cell; an egg cell or an egg apart from any investing membrane.

Palate—The roof of the mouth consisting of the structures that separate the mouth from the nasal cavity.

Population—A more or less separate (discrete) group of animals of the same species.

Posterior—Situated behind or to the rear; at or toward the hind end of the body (cf. Anterior).

Postocular—Behind the eye.

Postrostral scales—Scales between the rostral and internasals, as in certain rattlesnakes.

Predation—The act of capturing and killing other animals for food.

Predator—An animal that feeds by hunting and killing other animals.

Premaxillary teeth—Teeth attached to the premaxillary bones which are situated at the front of the upper jaw.

Prenasal—In rattlesnakes, the scale located immediately in front of the nostril.

Primitive—Of ancient evolutionary origin (cf. Advanced)

Species—A category of classification lower than a genus or subgenus and above a subspecies or variety; a group of animals or plants which possesses in common one or more characters distinguishing them from other similar groups, and which do or may interbreed and reproduce their characters in their offspring, exhibiting between each other only minor differences bridged over by intermediate forms (see subspecies) and differences ascribable to age, sex, polymorphism, individual peculiarity, accident, or to selective breeding by man; a distinct kind or sort of animal or plant.

Spectacle—The fixed transparent covering of the eye in snakes.

Subspecies—A subdivision of a species; a variety or race; a category (usually the lowest category recognized in classification) ranking next below a species. The differences separating subspecies are usually slight and are commonly bridged in zones of intergradation. Some systematists insist that intergradation should be the criterion in deciding whether two adjacent, slightly different animal populations should be considered as subspecies or species. If intergradation (or intermixture of characters) does not exist, they are regarded as species.

Substrate—The solid material upon which an organism lives.

Sympatric distribution—Overlapping or, in varying degrees, superimposed distribution of two or more subspecies, species, or higher categories. Relates to the coexistence (geographically) of two or more forms. (cf. Allopatric distribution).

Taxonomy—The science of classification; the arrangement of animals and plants into groups based on their natural relationships.

Temporal—Of or pertaining to the area of the skull behind the eyes (the temple).

Terrestrial—Living on land.

Thermoregulation—Control of body temperature by behavior and/or physiological means, such that it maintains a constant or near-constant value.

Translucent—Partly transparent; admitting passage of light but diffusing it, so objects beyond cannot be clearly distinguished.

Transversely—Crosswise; at right angles to the long axis of the body.

Vent—An outlet; the anal or cloacal opening of the body.

Venter—The underside of an animal including the tail.

Ventral—Pertains to the underside, or lower surface (belly), of the body.

Vertebral stripe—A stripe down the midline of the back overlying the position of the vertebral column.

Vertical pupil—An elliptical pupil with its long axis vertical.

Vestigial—Smaller and more simple structure than in an evolutionary ancestor.

Bibliography

Bakker, Elna S. 1972. *An Island Called California*. University of California Press, Berkeley, CA.

Banta, Benjamin H., and Alan E. Leviton. 1963. Remarks on the Colubrid Genus *Chilomeniscus* (Serpentes: Colubridae). Proceedings of the California Academy of Sciences 31(11): 309–327.

Barry, Sean J., Mark R. Jennings, and Hobart M. Smith. 1996. Current Subspecific Names for Western *Thamnophis sirtalis*. *Herpetological Review* 27(4): 172-173.

Basey, Harold. 1976. *Discovering Sierra Reptiles and Amphibians*. Yosemite Natural History Association, Inc.

Behler, John L., and F. Wayne King. 1979. *The Audubon Society Field Guide to North American Reptiles and Amphibians*. Alfred A. Knopf, New York.

Blaney, Richard M. 1973. *Lampropeltis. Catalogue of American Amphibians and Reptiles*. 150.1–150.2.

Brattstrom, Bayard H., and James W. Warren. 1953. A New Subspecies of Racer, *Masticophis flagellum*, from the San Joaquin Valley of California. *Herpetologica* 9(4): 177-179.

Briggs, Pat, and Sean McKeown, 1995. Natural and Captive Selected Color Phases of California Kingsnakes, (*Lampropeltis getula californiae*). *The Vivarium* 6(4): 26-29, 44-46.

Brode, John M. 1987. Natural History of the Giant Garter Snake, *Thamnophis couchii gigas*. In DeLisle, H. F., P. R. Brown, B. Kaufman, and B. M. McGurty (eds.), Proceedings of the Conference on California Herpetology. Special Publication No. 4, Southwestern Herpetologists Society, Van Nuys, CA.

Cole, Charles J., and Laurence M. Hardy. 1983. *Tantilla hobartsmithi. Catalogue of American Amphibians and Reptiles.* 318.1-318.2.

—— and ——. 1983. *Tantilla planiceps. Catalogue of American Amphibians and Reptiles.* 319.1-319.2.

Collins, Joseph T. 1990. *Standard Common and Current Scientific Names for North American Amphibians and Reptiles.* Third edition. Herpetological Circular No. 19. Society for the Study of Amphibians and Reptiles, Lawrence, KS.

DeLisle, H. F., G. Cantu, J. Feldner, P. O'Connor, M. Peterson, and P. Brown (eds.), 1986. The Distribution and Present Status of the Herpetofauna of the Santa Monica Mountains of Los Angeles and Ventura Counties, California. Special Publication No. 2. Southwestern Herpetologists Society, Van Nuys, CA.

Dixon, J. R., and R. R. Fleet. 1976. *Arizona, A. elegans. Catalogue of American Amphibians and Reptiles.* 179.1-179.4.

Ernst, Carl H. 1992. *Venomous Reptiles of North America.* Smithsonian Institution Press, Washington, D. C.

Fitch, Henry S. 1980. *Thamnophis sirtalis. Catalogue of American Amphibians and Reptiles.* 270.1-270.4.

——. 1983. *Thamnophis elegans. Catalogue of American Amphibians and Reptiles.* 320.1-320.4.

——. 1984. *Thamnophis couchii. Catalogue of American Amphibians and Reptiles.* 351.1-351.3.

Fowlie, Jack A. 1965. *The Snakes of Arizona.* Azul Quinta Press, Fallbrook, CA.

Frost, Darrel R. 1983. *Sonora semiannulata. Catalogue of American Amphibians and Reptiles.* 333.1-333.4.

Griffith, Donald D. 1966. *Snakes of California, Scientific and Common Names.* Herpeton 1(1). Southwestern Herpetologists Society, Van Nuys, CA.

Grinnell, J., and C. L. Camp. 1917. A Distributional List of the Amphibians and Reptiles of California. University of California Publications in Zoology 17(10): 127-208.

Grismer, L. Lee, Jimmy A. McGuire, and Bradford D. Hollingsworth. 1994. A Report on the Herpetofauna of the Vizcaíno Peninsula, Baja California, México, with a Discussion of its Biogeographic and Taxonomic Implications. *Bulletin of the Southern California Academy of Sciences* 93(2): 45-80.

Hahn, Donald E. 1979. *Leptotyphlops. Catalogue of American Amphibians and Reptiles.* 230.1–230.4.

———. 1979. *Leptotyphlops humilis. Catalogue of American Amphibians and Reptiles.* 232.1–232.4.

Halliday, Tim, and Kraig Adler (eds.). 1987. *The Encyclopedia of Reptiles and Amphibians.* Facts On File, New York.

Jeffrey, Charles. 1977. *Biological Nomenclature.* Edward Arnold (Publishers) Limited, London.

Jennings, Bryan. 1992. Personal communication.

Jennings, Mark R. 1983. *Masticophis lateralis. Catalogue of American Amphibians and Reptiles.* 343.1–343.2.

———. 1983. An Annotated Check List of the Amphibians and Reptiles of California. *California Fish and Game* 69(3): 151-171.

———. 1987. *Annotated Check List of the Amphibians and Reptiles of California.* Second edition, revised. Special Publication No. 3. Southwestern Herpetologists Society, Van Nuys, CA.

Kirk, James J. 1979. *Thamnophis ordinoides. Catalogue of American Amphibians and Reptiles.* 233.1–233.2.

Klauber, Laurence M. 1972. *Rattlesnakes: Their Habits, Life Histories, and Influence on Mankind.* Second Edition. University of California Press, Berkeley, CA.

Levell, John P. *A Field Guide to Reptiles and the Law.* 1995. Serpent's Tale, Excelsior, MN.

Liner, Ernest A. 1994. The Scientific and Common Names for the Amphibians and Reptiles of Mexico in English and Spanish. Herpetological Circular No. 23. Society for the Study of Amphibians and Reptiles, Lawrence, KS.

Loveridge, Arthur. 1945. *Reptiles of the Pacific World.* The MacMillan Company, New York.

McCleary, R. J. R., and R. W. McDiarmid. 1993. *Phyllorhynchus decurtatus. Catalogue of American Amphibians and Reptiles.* 580.1–580.7.

McCrystal, Hugh K., and Michael J. McCoid. 1986. *Crotalus mitchellii. Catalogue of American Amphibians and Reptiles.* 388.1–388.4.

McDiarmid, R. W., and R. J. R. McCleary. 1993. *Phyllorhynchus. Catalogue of American Amphibians and Reptiles.* 579.1–579.5.

McGurty, Brian M. 1987. Natural History of the California Mountain Kingsnake, *Lampropeltis zonata.* In DeLisle, H. F., P. R. Brown, B. Kaufman, and B. M. McGurty (eds.), Proceedings of the Conference on California Herpetology. Special Publication No. 4, Southwestern Herpetologists Society, Van Nuys, CA.

McKeown, M. Sean. 1997. Personal communication.

Medica, Philip A. 1975. *Rhinocheilus. Catalogue of American Amphibians and Reptiles.* 175.1–175.4.

Murphy, Robert W., Viera Kovac, Oliver Haddrath, G. Scott Allen, Alex Fishbein, and Nicholas E. Mandrak. 1995. mtDNA gene sequence, allozyme, and morphological uniformity among red diamond rattlesnakes, *Crotalus ruber* and *Crotalus exsul. Canadian Journal of Zoology* 73(2): 270–281.

Navy, U. S. Department of. 1965. *Poisonous Snakes of the World. A Manual for Use by U. S. Amphibious Forces.* U. S. Government Printing Office, Washington, D.C.

Parker, William S. 1982. *Masticophis taeniatus. Catalogue of American Amphibians and Reptiles.* 304.1–304.4.

Peters, James A. 1964. *Dictionary of Herpetology.* Hafner Publishing Company, New York.

Pickwell, Gayle. 1947. *Amphibians and Reptiles of the Pacific States.* Stanford University Press, Stanford, CA.

Pickwell, George V. 1972. *The Venomous Sea Snakes.* Fauna 1972(4): 17-32.

——, and Wendy A. Culotta. 1980. *Pelamis, P. platurus. Catalogue of American Amphibians and Reptiles.* 255.1–255.4.

——, Robert L. Bezy, and John E. Fitch. Northern Occurences of the Sea Snake, *Pelamis,* in the Eastern Pacific, with a Record of Predation on the Species. *California Fish and Game* 69(3): 172-177.

Price, Andrew Hoyt. 1982. *Crotalus scutulatus. Catalogue of American Amphibians and Reptiles.* 291.1–291.2.

Price, Robert M. 1990. *Bogertophis. Catalogue of American Amphibians and Reptiles.* 497.1–497.2.

Price, Robert M. 1990. *Bogertophis rosaliae. Catalogue of American Amphibians and Reptiles.* 498.1–498.3.

Rossi, John V., and Roxanne Rossi. 1995. *Snakes of the United States and Canada. Keeping Them Healthy in Captivity.* Vol. 2, Western Area. Krieger Publishing Company, Malabar, FL.

Rossman, Douglas A., Neil B. Ford, and Richard A. Seigel. 1996. *The Garter Snakes: Evolution and Ecology.* University of Oklahoma Press, Norman, OK.

Savage, Jay M. 1959. *An Illustrated Key to the Turtles, Lizards and Snakes of the Western United States and Canada.* Revised edition. Naturegraph Publishers, Happy Camp, CA.

Schätti, Beat, and Larry David Wilson. 1986. *Coluber. Catalogue of American Amphibians and Reptiles.* 399.1–399.4.

Schmidt, Karl P., and D. Dwight Davis 1941. *Field Book of Snakes.* G. Putnam's Sons, New York.

Schoenherr, Allen A. 1976. The Herpetofauna of the San Gabriel Mountains, Los Angeles County, California. Southwestern Herpetologists Society, Van Nuys, CA.

Scott, Norman J., Jr., and Roy W. McDiarmid. 1984. *Trimorphodon. Catalogue of American Amphibians and Reptiles.* 352.1–352.2.

—— and ——. 1984. *Trimorphodon biscutatus. Catalogue of American Amphibians and Reptiles.* 353.1–353.4.

Secor, Stephen M. 1994. Natural History of the Sidewinder, *Crotalus cerastes.* In Brown, Philip R., and John W. Wright (eds.), Herpetology of the North American Deserts. Special Publication No. 5, Southwestern Herpetologists Society, Van Nuys, CA.

Shaw, Charles E., and Sheldon Campbell. 1974. *Snakes of the American West.* Alfred A. Knopf, New York.

Spiteri, David G. 1987. The Geographic Variability of the Species *Lichanura trivirgata* and a Description of a New Subspecies. In DeLisle, H. F., P. R. Brown, B. Kaufman, and B. M. McGurty (eds.), Proceedings of the Conference on California Herpetology. Special Publication No. 4, Southwestern Herpetologists Society, Van Nuys, CA.

——. 1993. The Current Taxonomy and Captive Breeding of the Rosy Boa, *Lichanura Trivirgata. The Vivarium* 5(3): 18-34.

Stebbins, Robert C. 1954. *Amphibians and Reptiles of Western North America.* McGraw-Hill Book Company, Inc., New York.

——. 1972. *Amphibians and Reptiles of California.* University of California Press, Berkeley, CA.

——. 1985. *A Field Guide to Western Reptiles and Amphibians.* Second edition, revised. Houghton Mifflin Co., Boston, MA.

Stewart, Glenn R. 1977. *Charina, C. bottae. Catalogue of American Amphibians and Reptiles.* 205.1–205.2.

———. 1987. The Rubber Boa (*Charina bottae*) in California, with particular reference to the Southern Subspecies, *C. b. umbratica.* In DeLisle, H. F., P. R. Brown, B. Kaufman, and B. M. McGurty (eds.), Proceedings of the Conference on California Herpetology. Special Publication No. 4, Southwestern Herpetologists Society, Van Nuys, CA.

Sweet, Samuel S. 1997. Personal communication.

——— and William S. Parker. 1990. *Pituophis melanoleucus. Catalogue of American Amphibians and Reptiles.* 474.1–474.8.

Tennant, Alan. 1998. *A Field Guide to Texas Snakes,* 2nd ed. Gulf Publishing Co., Houston, TX.

Van Denburgh, John. 1922. *The Reptiles of Western North America.* San Francisco Academy of Sciences, San Francisco, CA.

Wareham, David C. 1993. *The Reptile and Amphibian Keeper's Dictionary: An A–Z of Herpetology.* Blandford, London.

Wilson, Larry David. 1973. *Masticophis. Catalogue of American Amphibians and Reptiles.* 144.1–144.2.

———. 1973. *Masicophis flagellum. Catalogue of American Amphibians and Reptiles.* 145.1–145.4.

———. 1978. *Coluber constrictor. Catalogue of American Amphibians and Reptiles.* 218.1–218.4.

———. 1982. *Tantilla. Catalogue of American Amphibians and Reptiles.* 307.1–307.4.

Wright, Albert Hazen, and Anna Allen Wright. 1957. *Handbook of Snakes of the United States and Canada.* Vols. 1 & 2. Comstock Publishing, Cornell University Press, Ithaca, NY.

Yingling, R. Peter. 1982. *Lichanura, L. trivirgata. Catalogue of American Amphibians and Reptiles.* 294.1–294.2.

Zweifel, Richard G. 1974. *Lampropeltis zonata. Catalogue of American Amphibians and Reptiles.* 174.1–174.4.

Index

M

Masticophis flagellum (8), 59, 60, 61, cp93, cp94
  masticophis flagellum fuliginosus 61
  masticophis flagellum piceus 61, cp93
  masticophis flagellum ruddocki 61, cp94, 186
Masticophis lateralis (9), 62, 63, 64, cp94
  masticophis lateralis euryxanthus 64, 186, 188
  masticophis lateralis lateralis 64
Masticophis taeniatus (10), 65, 66, cp95
  masticophis taeniatus taeniatus 65, cp95
Mojave rattlesnake (38), 12, cp120, 176, 177, 178
Mountain kingsnake, California (16), 82, 83, 84, 85, cp102, cp103

N

Night snake (31), cp114, 154, 155, 156
  California night snake 156
  desert night snake 156
  San Diego night snake 156
Northwestern garter snake (24), cp109, 138, 139

P

Patchnose snake, Western (11), 67, 68, 69, cp95
  coast patchnose snake 69
  desert patchnose snake 69
  Mojave patchnose snake 69
Pelamis platurus (32), cp114, 158, 159
Phyllorhynchus decurtatus (6), 53, 54, 55, cp92
  phyllorhynchus decurtatus perkinsi 55
Pit vipers (subfamily Crotalinae) 60

Pituophis catenifer (14), 75, 76, 77, 78, cp97, cp98, cp99
  pituophis catenifer affinis 77, cp97
  pituophis catenifer annectens 77, cp97
  pituophis catenifer catenifer 77, cp98
  pituophis catenifer deserticola 78, cp98
  pituophis catenifer pumilis 78, cp99
Protected species 61, 85, 136, 184, 185, 186

R

Racer (7), 56, 57, 58, cp92
  western yellowbelly racer 58, cp92
Rat snake, Baja California (12), 70, 71, cp96
Rattlesnakes
  Colorado Desert sidewinder 172
  Great Basin rattlesnake cp118, 175
  Mojave Desert sidewinder 172
  Mojave green rattlesnake 178
  Mojave rattlesnake (38), 12, cp120, 176, 177, 178
  northern pacific rattlesnake cp119, cp120, 175
  northern red rattlesnake 166
  Panamint rattlesnake cp116, 169
  red diamond rattlesnake (34), cp115, 164, 165, 166
  sidewinder (36), cp117, 170, 171, 172
  southern pacific rattlesnake cp117, cp118, 175
  southwestern speckled rattlesnake cp116, 169
  speckled rattlesnake (35), cp116, 167, 168, 169
  western diamondback rattlesnake (33), cp115, 162, 163
  western rattlesnake (37), cp117, cp118, cp119, cp120, 173, 174, 175
Red diamond rattlesnake (34), cp155, 164, 165, 166